THE POCKET PITCHING BIBLE

The Seven Secrets of a Perfect Pitch

Paul Boross

The Pitch Doctor

CGW
PUBLISHING

2012

THE POCKET PITCHING BIBLE

The Seven Secrets of a Perfect Pitch

First Edition: April 2012

ISBN 978-1-9082931-2-1

CGW Publishing 2012

Published by:

CGW Publishing
PB 1502
PO Box 15113
Birmingham
B2 2NJ
United Kingdom

www.cgwpublishing.com

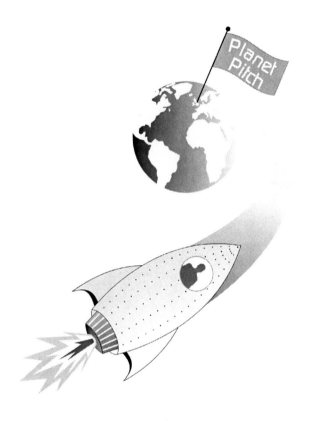

Welcome to The Pocket Pitching Bible, the companion guide to the best selling original, The Pitching Bible. This book is designed for anyone who needs to prepare, thoroughly and quickly, for an important pitch. This book is designed to get you there as quickly as possible whilst keeping all of the power of the Seven Secrets that you'll find in The Pitching Bible.

Contents

DIAGNOSIS: PITCH

Where Are You?

Let's begin by finding out where you are. You cannot get to where you want to be without first understanding where you are. And often, the biggest surprise is that you may not be exactly where you thought you were.

I want you to take time to seriously consider the following questions. Don't just skip through them. If you want to improve the success of your pitches, you have to work with me, with the emphasis being on "work". If you're not prepared to work at developing your pitching skills, you might as well give this book to someone who will make better use of it.

Work through the questions first before turning over to discover what your answers mean. Investing time in this part of the book will direct you to where your development priorities are, and that will save you time overall and bring you better results, faster.

1.1 Where are you?

1 When you think about putting your pitch together, what's the first thing you think of?

A: What I want

How I feel

What I need to say

B: What the client wants

How the client feels

What I want the client to do

2 When does your pitch begin?

3 What happens when you begin speaking?

4 How does the client feel at the end of your pitch?

5 What does the client do at the end of your pitch?

6 What does the client remember about your pitch?

7 What do you usually do after your pitch?

OK, let's see where we are.

1 When you think about putting your pitch together, what's the first thing you think of?

    A: What I want

         How I feel

         What I need to say

    B: What the client wants

         How the client feels

         What I want the client to do

If you answered "A" then your focus is on yourself, how you feel, what you want, what you're doing.

If you answered "B" then your focus is on your client, what they might be feeling, what they want, what they're doing.

Which is best? Well, it's not that simple. If you focus entirely on the client, you may give them what they want, but not achieve what you need. If you focus entirely on yourself then the client might as well not turn up to your pitch because you won't notice they're even there. A balance of both is vital for you to be focused on what you want to achieve *and* mindful of the real time feedback that your client is giving you. And since you need to aim your pitch squarely at your client's needs, the balance should tip in their favour. Your focus, as a general rule, should be on them.

If you answered "B", you can move on. If you answered "A" then your priority for development is in Secret 1, It's All About Them.

2 When does your pitch begin?

If you said something like "When I start to speak", or, "When I walk in the room", or even, "When I arrive at the office" then you need to work on Secret 2, By The Time You Start, It's Already Too Late.

The correct answer is, "The moment the audience buys the ticket"; the very first moment that they discover you will be pitching to them. This could be anything from minutes to months before you actually stand up in front of them, and it is the moment that the audience begins to form their preconceptions and expectations. If you don't influence how they form those expectations, you have missed an important opportunity to influence the outcome of the pitch.

3 What happens when you begin speaking?

Does it take a few minutes for the audience to settle down and give you their full attention? Are a few people still sneaking glances at their mobile phones? Do you feel that you have to repeat yourself, or wait for the audience to give you their attention? If so, you need to work on Secret 3, Steady, Ready, Pitch.

When you master Secret 3, the audience will have finished their settling down and will have given you their full attention before you begin speaking.

4 How does the client feel at the end of your pitch?

If your client feels doubtful, confused, uncertain or even just neutral and disengaged then you need to work on Secret 4, Dream The Dream.

Whatever you feel about your pitch; passion, excitement, curiosity, is what your audience will feel when you have mastered Secret 4.

5 What does the client do at the end of your pitch?

When you have finished the main, stand-up part of your pitch, what does the client do? Do they thank you and say they'll be in touch? Do they say that they have other proposals to consider? If so then you need to work on Secret 5, Mind Your Language.

When you master this secret, the end of your pitch will blur into the client's eager questions and clear desire for action.

6 What does the client remember about your pitch?

If the client can remember only bits and pieces of your pitch, if they get your pitch confused with someone else's, or if you kid yourself into thinking that if the client remembers only one key point then you've done a good job then you need to work on Secret 6, Say It Again, Sam.

If the client can clearly articulate the main points of your pitch, in fact, if they can sum up your pitch better than you could even do so yourself, then you have mastered Secret 6.

7 What do you usually do after your pitch?

After? You mean it ends?

If you go back to your office, get on with other things and wait for the client to get in touch then you have walked out on the pitch before it finished. The client continued turning things over in their minds and you failed to have any input into that vital reflective stage of the decision process. In this case, you need to work on Secret 7, The End... Or Is It?

If you rush back to your office so that you can get a follow up letter in the post the same day then that's an excellent start because you are influencing the client's reflective process so that they will remember more of what is most important. And if you follow up your letter with a call, and the client can't wait to meet you again, then you have finally mastered the Seven Secrets of a Perfect Pitch.

SECRET 1

IT'S ALL ABOUT THEM

What Do You Mean, It's All About Them?

A pitch requires three basic components; you, an idea and an audience. Without an idea, it's just a conversation. Without you, there's no-one to pitch. If you could get what you need all by yourself, you wouldn't need an audience.

The first thing to think about when you create your pitch is the audience and what you want them to do.

Sometimes, the right way to achieve a result is counter-intuitive. You can't make yourself relax, and professional athletes don't set out to win a race, they just focus on delivering their best. If they tried to win, their focus would be on their competitors which would distract them from giving their all.

When you pitch, you're aiming for the result that you want; perhaps to win the business, secure the investment or influence the decision. Yet none of these results is under your control, they all require the audience to do something. Yet paradoxically, you cannot make the audience do what you want, so while influencing the audience's behaviour is your desired outcome, it cannot be your focus.

Success is an outcome, an end result, not a primary aim.

1.1 Pitch Outcome

Let's start by setting an intention. Answer the following questions carefully.

What do you want?

Is that under your control?

What is the first step that is under your control?

How will you know when you have achieved it?

What will you see, hear and feel?

If I were to offer you that now, would you take it?

When your conscious and unconscious intentions are aligned, you achieve your goals almost effortlessly. The outcome exercise will help you to achieve that in anything that you set your mind to.

Mind and Body

Your unconscious mind automatically translates your intentions into actions. When you're worried, people notice. When you're stressed but trying to hide it, someone close to you knows how you feel because they can see that tell tale tension and hear the change in your voice. And when you've heard great news, everyone around you seems to know about it before you've told them.

In psychology, we call this reinforcing connection between mind and body a cybernetic loop, and you can master it to align your thoughts for success.

1.2 Cybernetic Loop

Think of a time when you felt really bad about yourself. Perhaps you really messed up an important pitch. Maybe you got into trouble at school. Think carefully about what happened and really immerse yourself in the memory.

Now pay attention to your body posture. What tension do you notice in your body? How are you breathing? What are you doing with your hands?

Now sit up straight, shoulders back, chin up, smile and try as hard as you can to remember that experience.

What's different?

Is it harder to remember the 'bad' memory?

You know that, if you smile while on the telephone, your voice tone changes. You also know that when you feel miserable, other people can see it because you sit and move differently. Your body betrays your thoughts, whether you like it or not.

Mind and Body Checklist

☑ Set an outcome to focus on the end result

☑ Focus on what is under your control so that your actions achieve that result

☑ Reinforce the thoughts that lead automatically to those actions

To get people to move in their minds, it's important to get them to move in their bodies. If a meeting is proving to be hard going, you can suggest that you all get some fresh air and a drink. Get people moving and their minds will move with you.

1.3 Checking Your Beliefs

Do this exercise in private so that you can be totally honest with yourself. If you're not, it won't help you.

Take a piece of paper and a pen or pencil and draw a square or rectangle to indicate the room that you'll be pitching in. Then draw two circles, one to indicate you and one for the audience you're pitching to.

Now mark a cross on the paper to indicate where you feel the centre of the drawing is. If that doesn't make sense, just go with your intuition.

Now, step back and look at the relative sizes of the shapes you have drawn.

If the 'room' is large compared to the piece of paper then you are leaving no room for anything else around the pitch. We often say that someone "blows something up out of all proportion" when they focus on one thing to the detriment of others.

If the 'room' is small compared to the piece of paper, then what do you imagine is in the space around it? You may be focusing too much on the pitch itself and on what happens in that room.

If the 'audience' is bigger than 'you' then you are placing the power in their hands, and you may unconsciously project a sense of inferiority, which is never a good quality in a business partner. Inferiority is not the same as respect; it is a submissive position. Even if you are pitching to many people, your relationship to them as an entity should be an equal one.

If the 'audience' is smaller than 'you' then you are in danger of being arrogant and projecting a sense of superiority. This is not the same as confidence; it is a dominant position.

If the circles are large relative to the 'room' then be careful not to attach too much significance to the pitch itself, and remember it is just one step in building the relationship. This could indicate that you are focusing too much on the pitch to the point of putting all your eggs in one basket.

If the circles are small relative to the 'room' or if 'you' are in the corner then this could indicate a fear of pitching, which is very common, entirely natural and easily overcome.

Finally, where is the cross?

If the cross is on or near to you, then the pitch is all about you, indicating that your focus may be too much on yourself and perhaps that means you're putting too much pressure on yourself and your performance.

If the cross is on or near to the audience, then the pitch is all about them, indicating that you are placing too much emphasis on the audience's power.

Where should the shapes be? They shouldn't be anywhere in particular, there is no right or wrong answer. This is merely a diagnostic exercise; use it to inform your preparation for your pitch by bringing your attention to your unconscious attitudes which will affect the outcome of your pitch.

This is also a useful tool to help you prepare for one to one meetings.

Now, I appreciate that it may be confusing that on one hand I'm saying "It's all about them" and on the other hand that focusing on the audience is not helpful either. How can both be true?

It's like asking whether the horse or the jockey wins the race. It's neither and both. Lawyers call this 'joint and several liability'. The jockey wants to win the race, but has to achieve that result with the horse's full cooperation. In a pitch, you want to get your desired result, but the audience has a goal too. You will achieve your objective through the audience, often by showing them how to achieve theirs.

Perception

Today, scientists and neurologists are fairly confident in their understanding of how the human brain perceives information and builds up a map of the outside world. The world contains information that we don't have the sensory organs to perceive, and what little is within our perceptual limits is usually outside of our awareness.

Simply, there is far too much information in the world around you, so your senses reduce that information so that you can more easily navigate around your environment.

The process of perception passes information through three layers of sensory filter which first delete, then distort and finally generalise incoming information in order to simplify it and make it fit your expectations.

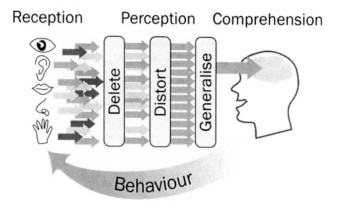

Reception   Perception   Comprehension

Delete   Distort   Generalise

Behaviour

What would it be like if you could modify your perception in order to more easily become aware of very subtle non-verbal signals from the client? Wouldn't that be useful? And what if you could direct your pitch through that narrow gap in the audience's perceptual filters?

When you pitch, your perceptions determine your performance, and part of that is understanding how your audience form their perceptions of you.

When the client has 'seen it all before', you're having to overcome those preconceptions before anything that you say or do will make any difference. The client has seen so many pitches that yours has to stand out. You may have thought that this was a bad thing, but actually this is a very good thing, and it's one of those counter-intuitive ideas that excellent pitchers take advantage of.

Ready, Aim...

1.4 Your Objective

Think of the last time that you presented, pitched or otherwise communicated with a potential customer with the intention of winning business.

What was your objective?

Now ask your colleagues what their objective is when they pitch.

The chances are that your objective was "to win the business".

That's the first mistake.

Many pitchers act as if this is the entire sales process:

Is it that simple?

1.5 Your Reasons

Think of the last pitch that you 'lost'.

Why did you lose it?

Was it:

A: Price, Competition, Market, Budget, Politics etc.

Or:

B: You personally did not do enough to 'win' it

When some people lose a pitch, they blame price, competition, a bad day or some other factor.

The only correct answer to exercise 1.5 is "B".

The sales process is not the simple two stage sequence that we saw previously:

Relationship >> Pitch >> Decision >> Win

You don't pitch to complete strangers. Some kind of relationship is already in place.

When you pitch to 'win', you are trying to control the outcome of the entire process, and that's not realistic. Focusing on winning means that you are avoiding accountability for what is under your direct control, so people who go all out to win are also the people you'll hear blaming the market, the presentation equipment, the client, their colleagues and their competitors. Their avoidance of accountability and control began the moment they set out to win.

What do you aim for then? You've already answered that question – in exercise 1.1.

Fire!

Once you are pitching to an audience, you are already on the short list, which means that, on paper, you can give them what they need. This is why I've said that the quality of your pitch is the single biggest factor in the success of your business.

Once you're standing in front of the audience, simply get on with the job at hand.

Get Your Focus Right

1.6 Focus

Answer these questions and count how many As and Bs you agree with. When you're pitching, do you:

Think about...

A: How you're feeling

B: How the audience is feeling

Rehearse...

A: What you're going to say

B: What the audience is going to do

Focus on...

A: Your opening line

B: Your closing line

Notice...

A: How you look

B: How the audience looks

Worry about...

A: Getting your point across

B: How the audience will respond

Think about what you want...

A: The audience to know

B: The audience to do

Focus on...

A: What the audience wants from you

B: What you want from the audience

If you answered mostly 'A's then your focus is on yourself.

If you answered mostly 'B's then you might be saying what you hope your pitches are like as opposed to what they are really like. It's remarkably difficult for us to focus entirely on other people, but a little bit of effort goes a long way.

There isn't a prize for getting this test right. There is only a prize for being honest about where you are right now, and that prize is the ability to master these Seven Secrets and become a more effective, more influential and more successful pitcher.

The first and most fundamental mistake that people make when pitching is that they focus on themselves.

Fear

A fear of public speaking is one of the most common problems in the world of business, yet it is easily solved. Here's one of the most valuable because when you try it out in your office, it looks exactly like you're practising your pitch, which is entirely normal.

1.7 Change Your Point of View

Remember a specific time that you presented and felt it went badly for you.

Many people remember their first big presentation, or perhaps something at school. When they are asked to prepare a pitch, they mentally re-run that first experience.

Second, mentally re-run your memory of the presentation as if you're watching a film, viewed through your own eyes. Relive exactly what you saw, heard and felt.

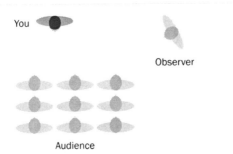

Remember looking out to the audience, starting just before the presentation starts to go badly and ending just afterwards. Recall the experience in as much detail as you can, making sure you have the sounds and feelings as well as what you saw. Really notice the sound of your voice and any feelings.

In between steps of this exercise, it's a good idea to take a short break. Just think about something else for a moment and then come back to the exercise.

Third, imagine yourself walking into the presentation room and sitting down as a member of the audience. Take a moment to look around you and see the other audience members.

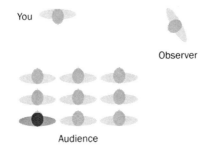

Look to the front of the room and see yourself presenting.

Watch and listen as you see yourself deliver the presentation and run a short film through from this new viewpoint. Pay attention to anything you notice at the point you thought it had "gone wrong".

Notice what you, in the audience, can see and hear. Notice how you feel about it.

Take another short break now. What colours can you see around you? What sounds can you hear? Who was the last person you saw on television?

Fourth, imagine yourself walking past the presentation room and stopping to peer in through the window.

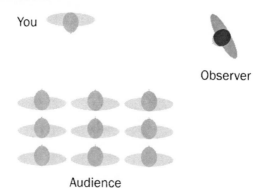

You can see both yourself presenting and yourself in the audience, and as you look from one to the other, you can see how they relate to each other. As you watch, you can run the sequence through again, and notice anything that you want to notice about it. For example, watch yourself presenting and see how the audience respond. Notice anyone in the audience who is nodding or frowning.

Take another short break now. What colour shoes are you wearing? What was the first thing you heard when you woke up this morning?

Now, bring what you've learned from these two new viewpoints back with you as you return to your starting point, standing at the front of the room, delivering the presentation.

Run the movie again, and this time pay close attention to how your feelings and perceptions have changed as a result of this new information. Use this new perception to rehearse the next presentation you will deliver, quickly in your mind.

This is a very important technique because:

☑ You can use it remedially, to solve problems

☑ You can use it to rehearse for future events

☑ It increases your metal flexibility, enabling you to see different points of view

☑ It will make you a better negotiator

☑ You can use it anywhere without drawing attention to yourself

On the next page is a list of some common fears and a simple prescription from The Pitch Doctor for each.

1.8 Fears

☑ If you think that people are looking at you then they are. It's why you're there.

☑ If you think that someone doesn't like you, then they probably don't. It's not why you're there.

☑ If you think you're going to fail, then you probably are, so take steps to change that.

☑ If you think you're going to be brilliant, remember that you're not there to give a performance.

☑ If you think you're going to forget what to say, then think what you want the audience to do.

☑ If you think that people aren't listening, then they're probably not, and neither would you be.

☑ If you think that the client doesn't like you, then realise they are giving you their time for a reason.

☑ If you think that people are bored, you don't know how they feel just from looking at them.

☑ If you think that people are being critical of you, then they might be, and why not?

☑ If you think that you're running out of time, look at the clock!

Give Yourself A Good Talking To

Self criticism can be another important source of fear. Ancient, irrational ideas play out in our minds and with no-one to act as a sounding board, the ideas just rattle around inside your mind, gathering momentum. If you actually spoke your fears or self criticism out loud, you could be sure that your friends or colleagues would say, "That's ridiculous!", or, "Who told you that?", or, "What on Earth would make you think that?"

1.9 Self Criticism

Think of a recent time when something went wrong, and you felt very self critical. Listen carefully to the voice you use to criticise yourself.

☑ Whose voice is it?

☑ What is it saying?

☑ How do you feel about it?

☑ What happens if you answer it?

☑ Answer with, "Shut up!" What happens?

☑ Answer with, "Thank you." What happens?

☑ Answer with, "Thank you. What do you suggest I do differently?" What happens?

Shift Happens

People learn fears quickly, and they can unlearn them just as quickly. What we first have to get through is the layer of reasons and excuses that keep the fear safe, because of all the fringe benefits it provides.

Letting go of fear is often about letting go of the sense of control that it affords, and once you can do that, you can unlearn the reaction you don't want and learn a new one very quickly.

Busy, Busy

If you use computer slides in your pitches and presentations then here's another test for you.

1.10 Slides

When you use computer slides in your pitch, do you:

A: Prepare too many 'just in case' and skip the ones you don't need during the pitch?

B: Prepare too few and use other means to get your message across if you need to?

If you answered 'A' then having too many slides is a sure sign that your focus is nowhere near your audience, that you're thinking more about what you want to say and less about what they need to hear.

The content of your slides is revealing, too.

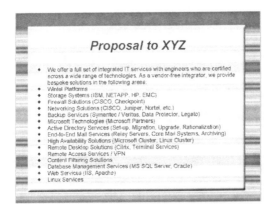

A slide like this guarantees that the presenter's focus is not on the audience, because it reveals that they are focusing on what they want to say, not on what the audience needs to hear.

This next slide was created to give the audience what they need to hear.

In general, try to pitch without using slides. Learn to deliver your pitch any time, anywhere, without having to rely on technology.

The Pitch Doctor's Top Tips

☑ Design your pitch *before* creating your slides.

☑ Create a slide *only* when you can't convey something in words alone.

☑ Create slides based on how you want the audience to *feel* and what you want them to *do*, not on what you want them to *know*.

☑ Create *half* the number of slides that you think you will have time for.

☑ When you have created your slides, ask a colleague to look through them. Don't say a word to explain. When they're finished, ask them what *story* they feel the slides tell. If you don't like what they say, then say "thank you" and change your slides.

☑ When you have finished your slides, go back and delete one quarter of them.

☑ And finally, if you are feeling brave, when you have finished creating your slides, delete the whole lot and learn to rely solely on the power of your own communication.

It's All About Me?

It's paradoxical, I know. You're pitching because of what you want, and your aim is to get the audience to do what you want them to do. So how can it be all about them?

The reason for your pitch is you.

The focus for your pitch is the audience.

People who fail generally have this back to front. They think that the audience is the reason for the pitch, and they focus on themselves. They think that they are pitching for the audience's benefit, or because the audience wants them to. They focus on themselves, their performance, their doubts, their fears. They focus on what they want to say, not on what they want the audience to do.

Remember, the reason that you are pitching is because you want something and the audience is your route to achieving it.

It's all about them because that's where your focus needs to be. Any fears or nerves will melt away when you focus on the audience.

Focus on the audience and you give yourself every chance of success.

Secret Brief

What Do You Mean, It's All About Them?

A pitch requires three basic components; you, an idea and an audience. Without an idea, it's just a conversation. Without you, there's no-one to pitch. If you could get what you need all by yourself, you wouldn't need an audience.

Mind and Body

Your mind and body are not separate entities; each one affects the other. You are a single system, and by changing the state of either your mind or your body, the other follows.

Perception

"Reality leaves a lot to the imagination" *John Lennon*

Ready, Aim...

Winning business is not the intention of your pitch, because that is not under your control.

Fire!

Once the pitch begins, you cannot control the end result. You can only control your behaviour and the decisions you make.

Get Your Focus Right

Most of the problems that you will ever encounter while pitching arise from the same source. It's also the reason that people become nervous when presenting. It's a focus on 'self' rather than 'audience'.

Fear

A fear of public speaking is one of the most common problems in the world of business. According to one survey, people fear it more than death. Fear is easy to overcome, if your focus is right.

Change Your Point Of View

If you are a nervous presenter, this simple and powerful exercise can help. It's also an excellent planning tool.

Give Yourself A Good Talking To

They say that talking to yourself is the first sign of madness. In fact, it's quite normal. We all have the capacity and need to converse with ourselves, and we can make some adjustments so that our internal conversations support our goals.

Shift Happens

Human beings learn very quickly.

Busy, Busy

Busy slides confuse the audience. While that may be your intention, generally it is not useful. Busy slides mean that your focus is on yourself, not your audience.

It's All About Me?

The reason for your pitch is you, the focus is the audience.

People who fail generally have this back to front. They focus on themselves, their performance, their doubts, their fears.

Remember, the reason that you are pitching is because you want something and the audience is your route to achieving it.

Therefore, it's all about them.

SECRET 2

BY THE TIME YOU START IT'S ALREADY TOO LATE

When Does the Pitch Begin?

What do you think?

Before you read any further, think this through for yourself.

Answer the question yourself, and ask some of your friends or colleagues what they think.

Hello! I said...

...answer the question

BEFORE you read any further...

OK. What was your answer?

Most people say something like:

☑ When you show the first slide

☑ When you stand up to speak

☑ When you walk into the room

☑ When the audience walks into the room

Try this for size:

The pitch begins when the audience buys the ticket.

Think about the last time you went to the theatre. The show began the moment you bought the ticket. When you made that commitment, you entered into a chain of events that created a compelling sense of anticipation in your mind, and that anticipation laid the foundation for the performance itself.

When you pitch, what is the moment that your audience 'buys the ticket'?

Setting the Scene

The pitch starts the moment the audience buys the ticket, the moment that they make a commitment to being part of the pitch.

From that moment on, everyone involved in the pitch is preparing themselves for it.

Consider these ideas for influencing the audience at the moment they 'buy the ticket':

☑ The title of your pitch

☑ How you word the invitation

☑ How you word the agenda

☑ The date and time of your pitch

☑ The timing of your pitch relative to other events

As You Enter the Theatre

When you pitch, what you say in your invitation tells the audience what to expect. If you don't send an invitation and just hope for the best, how can you expect to influence the events which follow?

The Invitation

☑ The purpose of the pitch

☑ Your intended outcome

☑ Who is invited and why

☑ What you want the audience to do

☑ Anything you want the audience to read or do

Some people still use 'power plays' such as inviting you to prestigious offices to make you feel inferior, or giving you a smaller chair than theirs. But why would they try to make you feel inferior? If you know you're superior, it doesn't even cross your mind to prove it, does it? So don't be influenced by such tricks, they are meant for your weak minded competitors.

The Lights Dim

In a cinema and theatre, the house lights make sure that the audience can see where they're going. They also mark out the start and end of the performance.

Starting Your Pitch: Don't

☒ Just start talking

☒ Start talking to the one person who is paying attention

☒ Interrupt the audience and ask if it's OK to start

Take control of the room from the moment you walk in

Starting Your Pitch: Do

☑ "It will take a few moments for us to get ready, please talk amongst yourselves until we let you know we're ready to begin"

☑ Lead the small talk while your colleague sets up

☑ Pause to allow the audience to clear their minds and give you their attention

Trailers and Adverts

Why do cinemas show trailers before the film and not afterwards?

If you're going to sell, do it while you have the audience's full attention. Do it as you're walking in to the room, as you're setting up your laptop, as you're waiting for the audience to settle down.

A visit to the cinema or theatre is not a random series of events but a process that has been carefully choreographed to capture your attention and lead you on a very predictable journey.

Your pitch must be just as carefully crafted, so let's look at how you might design your pitch, beginning, as always, with the end in mind.

Setting Out Your Pitch

Some people say that they never prepare, that they work best when they present 'off the cuff'.

What does 'off the cuff' actually mean? It actually means that they have written some notes on their shirt cuff. Which means that they prepared.

The people who do this are usually trying to impress others with their lack of any need for preparation. While other people are sweating over the details, they like to swan in at the last minute and impress everyone with their laid back attitude. However, this comes across as complacency and arrogance, and is very different to having the experience that allows you to step in and deliver a pitch at a moment's notice. People who have the confidence to do this have spent a lifetime preparing for every pitch.

Preparing for the pitch takes a number of important stages, so let's work through them, one by one.

Outcome

When you think about creating your pitch, what is your intention? What do you want to achieve?

To "inform the audience"?

To "tell them about my idea"?

To "hopefully...."

No!

In general, your outcome for a pitch should be to move your business a step forward in your overall business plan or strategy, whatever that may be. Even a "no" is better than "we'll think about it".

2.1 Setting an Outcome

When you want to set an outcome, ask yourself four questions:

☑ What do I want?

☑ How will the audience help me to get it?

☑ What do I need them to do for me?

☑ What do I need to do in order to achieve that?

If you're pitching in a team, sit down and work through these questions together.

It is very common for someone preparing a pitch to say that their goal is, "to win the pitch".

The problem with setting out to win a pitch is that:

☑ Winning isn't under your control

☑ Winning isn't clearly defined

☑ The pitch is not the prize

The pitch is not the prize

To be pitching means that you have already 'won the pitch'

Having the opportunity to pitch means that you have already 'won' the pitch.

You need to define precisely what it is you want to win, from whom and what the rules of the game are. The notion of 'winning' carries with it an element of competition. Although you may have competitors, you don't see many Olympic sprinters looking over their shoulders. The speed of their competitors is something that they cannot control, so they don't even worry about them.

Having said that 'winning' is not a particularly useful outcome, you're probably wondering what is?

Under Your Control

☑ Remembering what you're going to say

☑ Feeling relaxed and attentive

☑ Making good eye contact with everyone in the audience

☑ Enjoying yourself

☑ Pausing to think before choosing to answer any question

☑ Speaking in a clear and concise way

☑ Listening carefully to your client

☑ Wearing something appropriate to the situation

☑ Being on time

Your objective is not to win the pitch but to influence the client through their need for more information:

☑ They need to ask questions

☑ They want to see and hear the proposal, not just read it

☑ Facts alone are not enough

☑ They need to get a sense of 'you'

☑ They want to sense your passion for your pitch

☑ They want to find out if they like you

☑ If you don't believe in yourself, why would they?

☑ They need to interact with a real human being as part of their decision process

☑ They want to know that you really exist

Know the Rules

Your clients think in exactly the same way that you do. "We want suppliers to give us what we want, not what they want. And if you like the product so much, *you* buy it."

If you take the time to understand what the rules of their decision are, you have a better chance of focusing your efforts where they will make the biggest difference.

Psychologists[1] have long known that the reasons people give for decisions bear little relation to what actually went on in their minds when they made a choice. Therefore, asking the client what they're looking for in a product or service may not actually help you. You may achieve more by asking them *how* they'll weigh up those choices and how they need to *feel* about the decision they make.

When you first sit down to design and write your pitch, throughout the preparation process and as you're about to stand up and begin speaking, remind yourself of what it is that you want to achieve. This has to be your primary focus from start to finish, and because your means to achieve that is through the audience. It's all about them, as in Secret One.

---

1   From Change Blindness to Choice Blindness, Petter Johansson, Lars Hall and Sverker Sikström.

Audience

At this stage of the planning process, it's time to think about the audience, to understand who they are and why they are there.

Before the pitch, you need to ask the client who will be there. In fact, there are a few questions to ask:

Audience

☑ Name

☑ What is their role in the organisation?

☑ What is their role in the decision?

☑ What is their role in the implementation?

☑ What is their relationship to the other people involved in the decision?

☑ If present, how do you need to relate to them?

☑ If not present, how, when and what do you need to communicate to them?

☑ If they have not been involved up until now, what do you need to give them prior to the pitch?

☑ What follow up do they need after the pitch?

Knowing who isn't going to be there is important because if they're involved in the decision, you need to communicate with them. As a minimum, you need to send the 'ticket' and a follow up letter (which we'll talk about in Secret Seven).

Constraints

How long do you have for the pitch?

As a general rule, you should design your pitch to last between a half and three quarters of the time allowed. The worst thing to do is to try and cram as much in as possible. Focus on giving the absolute minimum required for the audience to make a decision. If they want more details, they'll ask.

Where will the pitch be held, and how much control do you have over the environment?

If the pitch will take place at the client's offices, can you see the room before the day of the pitch? It's easy to assume that all meeting rooms look the same, but you don't want to arrive and then find you're tripping over video conference equipment or that the room layout is for conferences and there's nowhere to stand so that everyone can comfortably see you.

What facilities and resources are there?

Do you need to take a projector, or do they have equipment built into the room? If you're going to use a flip chart or whiteboard, always take your own pens and make sure they work.

Subject

What will the subject be?

Does it centre around the product, or the client's problem, or the market opportunity?

The subject of your pitch might be your product, your company, the client's business problems, or something else. The subject is the main character around which you will build your story.

Angle

What's the 'angle'?

Is it how much money the client will save or how much they'll make?

The angle is the perspective of the main character in your story, from which the audience gains an insight into the subject. By choosing the angle, you influence how the audience feels about the subject.

Format

A traditional presentation?

An interactive demonstration?

A video?

The format of the pitch needs to make it as easy as possible for the audience to connect with the content.

Charts and figures would be good for venture capitalists, but perhaps not for creative directors. Product packaging samples might be good for marketing directors but not for technicians. Technical specifications might be good for technicians but not for investors. You get the idea.

Advertisers have, for many years, used the acronym AIDA when designing advertising campaigns:

☑ Attention – get the person's attention

☑ Interest – hold their interest

☑ Decision – get them to make a decision

☑ Action – get them to take action on that decision

It's certainly worth bearing AIDA in mind when you're designing your pitch.

Structure

Your pitch will tell a story, so you need to decide how you're going to organise the elements of that story.

There is no single format that you 'should' follow, only a format that most effectively tells your story and sells your idea or product.

Your pitch also needs to answer the audience's unspoken questions, which we'll come onto later.

When you plan the structure of your pitch, you also need to consider how you want the audience to feel or react at each stage. For example, at the beginning, do you want them to feel curious? Excited? Amused? Open? Nervous? In Secret Four, we'll explore what you do with these feelings.

Details

Once you have your structure worked out, fill in the details.

If you had started writing your pitch at the beginning and worked forwards, you would probably run out of time about two thirds of the way through your pitch.

By working on structure first and then adding in the details, you achieve two very important things.

Firstly, you can add in detail where you need it to support your pitch while staying within the time limitations, making your pitch very easy to edit once you start to practice it.

Secondly, you can respond seamlessly on the day of the pitch itself, when the client says, "Oh, I know we said you could have 30 minutes but we have to go to another meeting so could you do your pitch in five minutes?"

As you finalise the details for your pitch, you can create presentation aids such as computer slides and handouts. You can also decide what props you need, such as product samples, charts, models, videos etc.

Remember, starting with the structure first means that you can effortlessly move up and down in levels of detail to adapt to the available time, and the audience will perceive that your pitch was perfectly designed for the time available.

Opening

How will you open your pitch?

Many people focus on the opening, thinking that a big impression at the start will carry them through.

Unfortunately, there are two problems with this thinking. Firstly, creating an opening that has a different energy or direction to the rest of your pitch breaks rapport and does more harm than good. Secondly, this approach is all about you. By putting your focus on yourself and your big opening, your focus is no longer on the audience.

People often employ a high energy opening as a way of overcoming the barrier that their own fear presents. This is a clear indication of a focus on themselves, because if they were focused on the audience, there would be no fear, no barrier, and no need for all that energy.

Closing

Closing serves three important purposes; it wraps up any loose ends from your pitch, it drives home your main message and it marks the point where you hand the room back to the audience.

Once of the most important considerations when closing your pitch is how to handle questions. What most people do is to close their pitch and then permit questions. This is a mistake because it hands control of the pitch back to the audience. I'll cover this in more detail in Secret Seven, but for now, design your pitch so that you place a Q&A section within your pitch, and close afterwards. Even if your close is only ten seconds, that is preferably to allowing your pitch to fizzle out when the audience can't think of any more questions.

Roles

Who is doing what? If you're pitching by yourself, you don't have to do it alone. You have friends and colleagues who can help with the design and practice stages, even if you're the only person to stand up in front of the client.

Once you know who is doing what, you need to brief them so everybody understands, as an absolute minimum:

☑ The outcome for the pitch

☑ What you are proposing to the client

☑ Who you are pitching to

☑ Their role and responsibility

When a pitch involves a large project team, it can be tempting to have everyone there in case of questions, and it all depends on the nature of the pitch. Sometimes, it would be fine for you to have a whole team of experts with you. At other times, there's no other option than for you to stand alone. Whether your pitching team is one or ten, the aim is the same – to speak with one voice.

Send the Ticket

Now it's time to send the ticket. This could just be an agenda, but I recommend that you write a letter of invitation to each person involved in the decision.

Remember that what the client reads before the pitch sets their expectations. When you arrive and see them in the room, they have bought the ticket, they have accepted your invitation and they have a reason to be there.

Practice

Practice until you are confident that you understand your pitch inside out. Do not practice until you think you can control the outcome, because you have no idea what the audience is going to do and your focus needs to be on the people you are pitching to.

It's also very important, if you're using slides, to know the running order and plan ahead. If you show the next slide and have to stop and read it yourself in order to know what to say, the audience is already ahead of you.

'Mental rehearsal' is a technique used by athletes and entertainers as a way of setting a complex activity into their minds as if it were a memory of something they have already done.

It involves using all of your senses and imagining going through the entire experience, seeing, hearing, feeling and even tasting and smelling if those are relevant.

2.2 Mental Rehearsal

Feel the floor beneath your feet, feel your muscles move confidently as you look up at the audience, feel your mouth open, hear your voice, feel your smile, see the audience smiling and nodding and feel a comfortable sense of accomplishment as you hear yourself ask, "I'd like to take a few questions from you before I close my pitch".

The important thing about mental rehearsal is that you must not imagine the outcome, because to have a mental script for what other people will do means that you're trying to control the outcome.

Racing drivers mentally rehearse a race track but they can't plan for what the other drivers are going to do. Therefore, they rehearse the twists and turns of the track to make it familiar, so that they can concentrate more on the other drivers during the race. They rehearse the track, not the race.

Athletes rehearse the track, not the race

Pitch Design Reminder

Design

- ☑ Outcome: What do want to achieve?
- ☑ Audience: Who are you pitching to?
- ☑ Constraints: Time? Space? Resources? Facilities?
- ☑ Subject: What is the subject of your pitch?
- ☑ Message: What is the one message you want the audience to have firmly in mind?
- ☑ Format: Product demo? Video? Q&A?
- ☑ Structure: How will you organise your pitch into a journey or story, influencing the audience's state?
- ☑ Angle: What's the angle? Who are you telling the story to? Who are you telling it as?
- ☑ Details: What are the details for the pitch, to fit into the structure, given the time constraints?
- ☑ Opening: How will you open your pitch, creating curiosity and a desire to learn more?
- ☑ Closing: How will you close your pitch, leaving the client with your primary message?
- ☑ Roles: Who is doing what during the pitch?
- ☑ Send the Ticket: Send the audience the invite, the teaser, the sample, the trailer, 'the ticket'.
- ☑ Practice: Practice until you understand your pitch

If a pitch isn't worth preparing, it isn't worth delivering

Personal Outcome

In addition to an outcome for each pitch, you can also have a personal outcome which you can achieve, regardless of the actual result of any individual pitch.

Your personal outcome might be something like:

☑ To notice when the audience gives their attention

☑ To feel more in control than you did before

☑ To learn something valuable for your next pitch

When you set a personal outcome for yourself, you achieve an overall direction for your pitches that helps you to consistently improve your skills and increase your success rate.

Tickets Please!

The eager anticipation that you feel just before the curtain goes up or the lights dim is right there, waiting in every audience you pitch to, if you let them know that they're in for a very special experience.

How do you let them know that's what to expect?

Get them to buy a ticket.

Secret Brief

When Does the Pitch Begin?

Your pitch doesn't begin when you say your first word, or when you show your first slide, or even when you walk into the room. Your pitch begins the moment the audience buys the ticket.

Setting the Scene

A lot happens before anyone has set foot in a meeting room or clicked on 'File...New...' and your audience is already waiting for you to walk onto their stage.

As You Enter the Theatre

The environment creates its own expectation.

The Lights Dim

When it's time to begin, your audience's attention shifts onto you. This is the moment when you take control of the room.

Trailers and Adverts

Don't launch straight into your pitch. Think about how you can entice the audience to join you on your journey.

Setting Out Your Pitch

When you are ready to design your pitch, follow these steps to make sure you have covered every angle and anticipated as much as possible.

And remember, if a pitch isn't worth preparing for, it isn't worth delivering.

Personal Outcome

As well as an outcome for the pitch itself, you can have a personal outcome which you can achieve, regardless of what the client's decision is.

Tickets Please!

Every audience waits to be enthralled. All they need is a ticket.

SECRET 3
STEADY
READY
PITCH

Making a Connection

Have you ever listened to someone and thought, "Why are you telling me all this?"

Making a Connection Checklist

Don't

☒ Just start and hope the audience will catch up

☒ Tell an inappropriate story

☒ Tell a joke at anyone's expense

☒ Tell a joke – play it safe!

☒ Hide behind a lectern or desk

Do

☑ Smile, it helps you to relax

☑ Make *relevant* small talk

☑ Start with generalisations

☑ Have a colleague set up as you talk to the client

☑ Surprise the audience

☑ Tell an engaging story

☑ Pause

☑ Wait for the audience to settle and look at you

☑ Smile some more, it lets the audience relax

The same thing happens when you launch into your pitch. The client is thinking, "What's going on? Why are they telling us all this?" Before you get to the main 'body' of your pitch, you must allow the audience to 'tune in'. That's what making a connection with them is all about.

State

3.1 How do you usually feel when you are about to begin a pitch?

Excited?

Nervous?

Apprehensive?

Confident?

Happy?

Where do these feelings come from?

Do you always remember to feel this way?

Do you imagine how the pitch is going to end before you deliver it?

Do you remember this diagram?

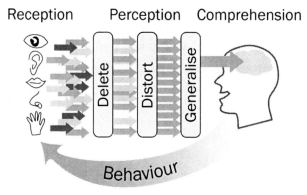

When you first saw it, you might have wondered how it might be possible to influence the perceptual filtering process so that the information that you want to receive gets through.

Your perceptual filter is the window through which you interact with the outside world. We normally act as if our perception *is* the world, rather than a pared down, twisted, simplified representation of it.

We could say that a person's response to external events is a good description for their 'attitude'. Your attitude is the way that you face the world, and it is based on your reactions to your limited perceptions. We could also use the words 'attitude', 'feeling' and 'state' interchangeably in some circumstances.

So if you had a way to control your state, you would control your attitude and you would have more control over external events.

Anchoring

Anchoring is simply a technique based on our natural ability to make connections. It is the process by which we can attach a stimulus, such as the sound of a piece of music, to a response, such as a particular memory or feeling that it reminds you of.

3.2 Making Connections

You might be familiar with the kind of puzzle where you have to change a word from PITCH to BIBLE, one letter at a time.

In this exercise, start by thinking about your first day at school and for the next two minutes, notice where your thoughts take you, linking from one to the next.

Now look around you and choose an object that you can see. Repeat the exercise, starting with an event that this object reminds you of.

What do you notice about the connections that you have made?

If you prefer, have a friend or colleague make notes as you call out a reminder for each memory that you move to.

Incidentally, can you get from PITCH to BIBLE, changing only one letter at a time? One solution can be found in the Appendix.

And could you use concept this to design you pitch, leading the audience smoothly from your start to your finish, like a journey that's brought you safely to your destination before you've even realised it?

3.3 Anchoring

1. Choose a state that you want to experience
2. Think of a specific time when you felt this way
3. Review the experience and find the trigger moment

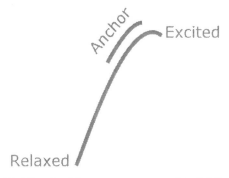

4. Replay the trigger moment and build the state
5. Find a word, colour, image, sound etc. that seems to fit the state
6. Break your state by bringing yourself back to your current environment
7. Repeat steps 4 to 6, noticing how the state builds intensity
8. Break state completely
9. Test the anchor by saying the word, imagining the colour, image or sound etc.

Rapport

Rapport is the invisible connection between two people; a communication medium through which you can convey your thoughts, ideas, intentions, hopes, dreams and fears.

Rapport Checklist

Don't

☑ Stand behind a barrier such as a lectern

☑ Give all your attention to one person

☑ Turn your back on the audience

☑ Talk to the slides or whiteboard

☑ Hide in the corner

☑ Argue with your colleagues

☑ Lie about your intentions

Do

☑ Let your audience see you

☑ Smile

☑ Pause before beginning to speak

☑ Make eye contact

☑ Be honest

☑ Get close to the audience, but not too close

☑ Nod

☑ Keep smiling!

We are always communicating, whether we like it or not, and this is why pitching something that you don't believe in is often fruitless. Your whole being will communicate your real feelings, even if the audience can't quite figure out why you're not being sincere.

Listen to the conversations around you, and you'll hear the word "but". "Yes, but" is not an agreement, it is a disagreement, and that means a break in rapport which means a lost connection with the audience, and you know exactly what that means.

"But" means "except". I agree with you, except... which means that I don't agree with you at all.

It's easy to say "don't say but", and you can certainly try. The problem is that saying "but" reveals that, in your heart, you do disagree. When someone says, "I agree with you, but", or "yes, but", you're more than likely to take that to mean, "I feel that I should say I agree with you, but really I don't".

The word "but" implies that there is only one point of view, and you can learn to avoid it by getting the idea firmly in your mind that anything said by any person, ever, is a statement of their experience, not a definition of reality. It's impossible to disagree with someone else's experience, it's only possible for yours to be different.

If a friend of yours likes a particular style of music and you think it's terrible, are they wrong? If they are, then you're not much of a friend! Now, some people have learned that their thoughts are universal, objective. They say, "That music is terrible, no-one really likes it, you shouldn't listen to it, turn it off". Other people have learned that their thoughts are individual, subjective. They say, "I don't really like that music. Do you mind if we put something on that we can both enjoy?"

Appreciating the world as a subjective place means that there are far more possibilities than those which you have already experience. It means becoming a curious, inquisitive and insightful person.

3.4 Ifs, Buts and Monkey Nuts

When you hear something that you disagree with:

1. Pause

2. Notice how interesting it is that someone could have that point of view - it means that the subject is bigger than you had previously thought

3. Say, "Yes, and..."

4. Enjoy the difference

Another word that breaks rapport is "no". Hearing it can even be a physical sensation, like walking into a brick wall. And the more you want something, the harder it is to hear the word.

Some sales people work in very challenging environments, for example in public places, selling credit cards and other services. It's challenging because they have to deal with an enormous amount of rejection, and so they become very resistant to the word, "no", to the point of ignoring it completely. Their rule of thumb is that if someone is still standing there, they don't really mean "no", they mean, "not yet". This approach might work in the street, but I don't recommend it for your pitch. Be tenacious, but when the answer is no, back off and take a different route.

3.5 No

"No" is a dead end. It cuts the conversation off and offers no way forwards.

At work, instead of saying "no", try this:

"Yes, if"

This is a negotiation.

Try it and see what happens.

Breaking rapport is not always a bad thing. It can, in fact, be an excellent way to get someone's attention. Once you have rapport, breaking it creates tension, and people naturally need a way to release that. Laughter is probably the most common way of releasing that tension, but that is not always appropriate, so you break rapport, it is important to reconnect with a smile and a clear way forward.

3.6 Testing Rapport

Find a partner who can help you for 20 minutes with this exercise.

First, find four conversation subjects, two that you broadly agree on and two that you disagree on. For example, you might choose topics such as sport, films, cooking, politics or foreign travel.

Sit comfortably, facing each other with a full view of each others' body posture. Don't have anything like a table between you.

Notice how your partner is sitting so that you can adjust your posture to match or mismatch theirs when necessary. For example, notice where their arms and legs are, where their feet are pointing, how their hands are resting, the angle of their head and shoulders, their facial expression and their angle in the chair.

This exercise is in four stages, each one taking five minutes. Adjust your posture and then begin a conversation on the chosen subject.

1. Match posture, agree on the subject

2. Mismatch posture, disagree on the subject

3. Mismatch posture, agree on the subject

4. Match posture, disagree on the subject

At the end of each stage, note how you both feel about each other and the subject.

At the end of the whole exercise, note how you both feel overall and what you each noticed.

Did you notice that, when you were mismatching, you found things to disagree about, even for a subject that you thought you agreed on? And did you find that, for a subject that you disagree on, you found a different point of view when you matched postures?

Whilst agreement builds rapport, being in rapport with someone definitely does not mean that you automatically agree with them, and it doesn't mean that they will automatically agree with you. At best, it means that you both become open to other points of view, and that in itself is extremely valuable in a pitch.

3.7 The Dance of Rapport

After you have spent some time observing your colleagues, you will probably notice that some of them show their feelings much more readily than others. When people agree with them, they match and reinforce that agreement, when people disagree they mismatch very strongly, almost trying to make the other person feel bad for not agreeing with them.

Choose one of these people, and next time you're in a meeting or conversation with them, play devil's advocate. Switch between two opposing points of view as if weighing up the options and notice the dance that they perform for you as they alternate between trying to make you feel good for agreeing with them and bad for disagreeing with them. End by leaning towards agreement and then saying that you can't make your mind up.

Group Rapport

How do you get rapport with a group?

The simplest answer is don't bother. If you are congruent and open, you will find that a group or audience gradually gets into rapport with you. Their states will converge on yours, with more influential people in the group, rapport leaders, moving first.

If you concentrate your attention on those rapport leaders, you risk alienating other people, and often, the most powerful people in a room are the quietest.

I'm Sorry, I'm Losing You

What happens if you lose rapport during your pitch?

☑ Do you stumble on and hope for the best?

☑ Do you do something to get the audience's attention?

☑ Do you stop?

How you deal with it is very much down to your personality, and nothing else. How you deal with it is not about what's appropriate for the audience or right for that client, it's all down to how comfortable you are in dealing with people who are being disrespectful to you.

The only important thing is that you do deal with it, otherwise it just distracts you and damages your pitch, because anything that distracts you will break rapport and disconnect you from the audience.

Emergencies will no doubt arise at some point during a pitch, but if someone gets a genuinely important message, they can leave the room to deal with it, especially if you give them permission to do that at the start of your pitch, as we talked about earlier.

A good way to deal with interruptions is to pre-empt them, thereby bringing them to the audience's attention, and you'll find any remaining distractions much easier to handle.

> "In a moment we're going to begin our pitch, so I just wanted to let you know that I appreciate you're busy, and during the 20 minutes we're going to be speaking, I'm asking you for your undivided attention, and in return we're going to stick to what is most relevant and important to you, based on the information you have given us. If you get an urgent message that you need to take care of, feel free to go and do that so that it's out of your mind and when you're here in the room, you're as fully focused on this as we are."

Influence

Rapport is a two way communication process. You signal your state of mind to other people and they signal theirs back to you.

And therein lies the problem. While you're influencing them, they're also influencing you.

When you genuinely believe that a business relationship will be mutually beneficial, rapport and influence will never be a problem for you.

Territory

Good presenters begin by marking out their territory as they enter the room.

When you walk into a meeting room, you have a right to be there, and you have earned that right fair and square. You didn't trick your way past the security guard. You didn't drug the real presenter and take his or her place at the last minute. You didn't sneak in through the window.

3.8 The Pitching Space

Try this experiment with a few colleagues.

Go into a presentation room in your office and tell them that there's going to be a 5 minute presentation that you want their feedback on. This will get them to sit as if they expect someone to present. Sit with them as a member of the 'audience'.

What happens?

How do they interact with each other?

More importantly, how do they interact with the empty space at the front of the room?

Presenters who dodge around at the front of the room, who back away from the audience and who hide behind lecterns and flip chart stands gain no respect from the audience. It's as if the audience threw them a hot potato and they do their best to get rid of it. Since they don't want control of the space, the audience ultimately takes it back.

It is vital that you are ready to accept control of the presentation space, and that you only hand it back when you are ready to do so, on your terms. We'll explore how you do this in Secret Seven.

A presentation room without a presenter is like a living room with the TV switched off. Everyone looks at the front of the room, hoping that something interesting will happen if they stare for long enough.

3.9 Claiming the Space

If your colleagues are willing to indulge your experiment for a few minutes longer, here's part two.

Go and stand at the front of the room, in the presenter's space, but say and do nothing. Just look at the audience.

Stay there for much longer than feels comfortable and notice how you feel, then sit down and ask your colleagues how they felt.

Notice how their comments relate to their uncertainty about who was in control.

What can you deduce from this experiment?

When people sit in a room and face a screen or even an empty space, they look for someone to give control to, to listen to, to learn from.

This isn't an innate behaviour that you were born with, it had to be learned, most likely at school.

The more the situation feels like 'being taught', the more some people behave like school children. This is another one of those preconceptions that your pitch must break through.

Behaviours or 'roles' that you can observe include:

☑ The teacher's pet, sitting at the front, taking copious notes, asking questions and not having a clue what's really going on

☑ The rebel, sitting at the back, sniggering and trying to attract other people's attention

☑ The class know-all, trying to correct the presenter because they know better

☑ The class idiot, acting dumb because they fear they *are* dumb

☑ The class clown, joking to draw attention away from their lack of understanding

☑ The class supervisor, disapproving of their colleagues' behaviour

☑ The class swot, writing everything down, asking questions, listening intently, ignoring colleagues

3.10 Class Wars

Which of these behaviours have you observed?

Which have you engaged in?

As a presenter, how do you respond to them?

Find some colleagues who have experience of presenting and ask them the same questions.

How can you learn to deal with disruptive people?

Are 'nice' people (teacher's pet, swot, clown) the hardest to deal with?

All of these disruptive behaviours are designed to get attention. Unfortunately, in order for you to get your message across, you need the audience's attention. Any member of the audience who competes for attention will prevent you from achieving your outcome.

I know that it can be uncomfortable to deal with these disruptions, so I don't blame you if you avoid the potential conflict because I have done it myself. And as a direct result, I lost control of the pitch and lost the business. What happens in your pitch is entirely up to you. The only crime is not learning from your mistakes.

Making an Impression

When you walk into the room, the audience will make their minds up about you in two to three seconds. In one glance, they will assess your credibility, social status, emotional state and intentions.

The non-verbal information that you radiate will lay the foundation for everything that happens from the moment you enter the room. We have also talked about the concept of mental rehearsal, and how you can prepare yourself for the pitch in the way that professional athletes prepare for a race.

91%

91% of employers[2] equate an applicant's dress and grooming with their attitude towards their potential employer. 95% equate the applicant's suitability for the job with their appearance.

---

2   Jobweb.com annual survey, 2002

The way you look is important, not because I say so but because your potential client will draw a conclusion from it, and on that conclusion, they will base their decision to buy from you.

3.11 First Impressions

Have you ever made up your mind about someone just from the way that they looked?

Why?

Do you think people have done the same to you?

Has that always worked in your favour?

You are not pitching to express your individuality, to impress with your style orto find a romantic partner.

You are pitching to secure a business relationship.

Dress accordingly, even if it's not how you dress at the weekend.

If you were visiting a building site, would you refuse to wear a hard hat, because the colour would clash with your suit?

The audience is not interested in your sense of fashion

They are only interested in doing business with a fellow professional

Non-Verbal Communication

Incongruence is a state of misalignment between something and its context. For example, an elephant wearing ice skates is incongruous.

In 1969, the social psychologist Albert Mehrabian and his assistant Michael Argyle performed a study which is probably the best known work ever carried out on communication and influence.

Mehrabian and Argyle gave subjects words and phrases to read to each other and paired those words with different intonations and facial expressions. They deduced that the overall meaning that we take from a message is a combination of factors; some verbal (words) and some non-verbal (tone, pitch, facial expressions, gestures).

The result of Mehrabian and Argyle's work is this famous pie chart:

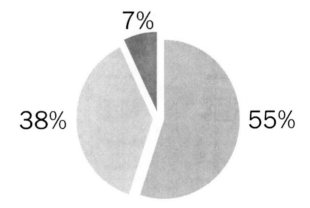

Visual Non-Verbal	Tonal Non-Verbal	Verbal
55%	38%	7%
Facial expressions	Pitch	Words
Hands	Volume	
Body	Intonation	
	Pace	
	Rhythm	

Not everyone agrees with these figures, and some people even dispute the original research. I just want to make it clear that words are not the only form of communication between human beings. However, it's important to bear in mind that words only make up 7% of *meaning*, and meaning can change dramatically, even just with a subtle change in voice tone or the raise of an eyebrow. The word "hello" could *mean*, "You're late again", "I'm pleased to see you", or "Would you like to come and see my etchings?", with only subtle changes in the *way* the word is spoken.

If you want to check the figures for yourself, it's always best to conduct your own, independent research. Here's how.

3.12 Non-Verbal Communication

You'll need a group of people for this, perhaps ten or more. It's also best to have a presenter who isn't well known to the group.

Ask someone to present for 20 seconds on a subject of their choosing. Ask the group to write down the first five things that they notice.

After 20 seconds, stop the presenter and ask everyone to count their observations.

Make a note of the number of:

Things they saw

Things they heard, as in specific words

Things they heard, as in voice tone, pauses, accent, ums and ahs etc.

Total everyone's figures up and work them out as a percentage of the total.

Let's say that your numbers are 78 'saw', 62 'tone' and 9 'heard'. Add them all together, that's 149. Now divide each one into the total, so that's 78/149 = 0.52 for 'saw'. That's 52% of the overall communication.

In this example, 'tone' is 42% and 'words' are 6%.

If you want to draw a pie chart, just multiply your results by 12 and draw imaginary hands on a clock face. That puts 'saw' at about half past six, 'words' at just past eleven o'clock and 'tone' is the space in between. Easy!

In all the dozens of times I've done this experiment during training courses, these figures are very typical. The only thing that really affects the 'words' figure is when the presenter is speaking about a subject that is very relevant to the group, for example on a very hot day when the presenter was talking about ice cold beer. Everyone heard the words "cold beer"!

Incongruence results from a conflict between any or all of these three components of communication. For example, with a smile on their face, your boss tells you that they're sorry but they've got to let you go. Or, with wide eyes and shaking hands, your partner tells you that they're fine.

You know that there's something missing, you just don't know what.

Aside from a simple nod or shake of the head, the non-verbal components of communication provide the context within which we make sense of the verbal component. The overall *message* that the person intended to give you is a combination of the two.

When your audience detects incongruity, people may not recognise it consciously but they will still find it hard to accept what you say. When you're in an incongruent state, you're more likely to generate confusion and doubt in other people.

3.13 Getting the Message

If you're at a presentation in the near future, take a few minutes to observe every single part of the speaker that communicates part of his or her overall message. Observe their eyes, eyebrows, hands, fingers, shoulders, legs, feet, breathing, mouth, cheeks, head, everything that you can.

Make a list of each component and, looking at it in isolation, work out what message they are conveying and if their communication is congruent.

If you don't have a presentation to attend, watch the unscripted interviews on an extended news and current affairs TV program.

An imbalance in your own thoughts and intentions is communicated over multiple channels, all of which are received and processed by your audience. The result is that they feel the same unease, the same conflict, and they attribute that to you. Rapport turns out to be a double edged sword. Without it, you communicate nothing. With it, you communicate everything, whether you intend to or not. You can't hide anything when you're in rapport.

What is actually happening is that there is not one single communication channel between two people, or between one person and an audience. Every part of your body that can convey information does convey information, constantly.

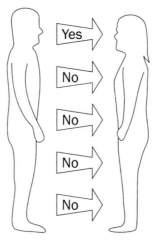

Don't try to force or contrive your body language. Non-verbal communication is far too complex to make it up as you go along, which is why it's so valuable for you to observe in other people.

When your words, voice, eyes, hands and body all communicate the same information, your message is reinforced and your audience will receive it, loud and clear. You could say that you're speaking from your head and heart at the same time, and no-one can fake that.

Eye Movements

Interpreting non-verbal communication is the subject of an entire book in itself, so I'm going to cover just some of the aspects that are most practical for considering when you're pitching, one of which is eye movement.

Our thoughts are a constant stream of information, some external and some internal. When we are processing internal information, we could call that 'thinking', and when we think, we use the same parts of our brain as we use for taking in new, external information.

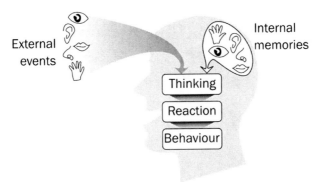

We think using our senses, and since every memory, thought and experience can be broken down into an image, sound, feeling taste or smell, we have a very useful way to understand how people think.

When people think, their eyes tend to move automatically. Experts have no idea why this happens, but you can often observe consistent patterns. For example, if someone makes a mental image, they tend to look up.

3.14 Eye Movement

Find a colleague to help you with this exercise.

Memorise each question and then look the person right in the eye as you ask it. If you read from the page, you will miss the eye movement as it will happen as soon as the person understands the question, long before you have finished reading it.

◇ What colour is your bedroom ceiling?

◇ Where is the bed in relation to the window?

◇ When you pull back the curtains, what sound do they make?

◇ How would they sound if you pulled them faster?

◇ What do they feel like?

◇ How does it feel to walk in snow?

◇ What sound does it make?

◇ How does a paper cut feel?

◇ How does your favourite person's voice feel?

◇ Say to yourself, "Mary had a little lamb"

◇ Say to yourself, using the voice of a favourite cartoon character, "Mary had a little lamb"

◇ What's the thing you enjoy doing most?

Observing someone's eye movements when you ask them a question gives you an insight into how they are organising their thoughts, and that in turn tells you how best to communicate with them, which is something we'll be exploring in detail in Secret Five.

Credibility

Can you believe that we're almost at the point where you're going to open your mouth and say your first words? Can you guess what they might be?

As a social species, one of the things that we need to ascertain about any stranger is their intentions, and so the first question on the audience's mind is:

"Who are you and what do you want?"

The answer to that question is where you gain credibility.

The audience's other unspoken questions can include:

☑ Do we have anything in common?

☑ Do I like you?

☑ Do I believe you?

☑ Do I trust you?

☑ Do you believe yourself?

☑ Do you know what you're talking about?

☑ Is this relevant to me?

☑ Do I respect you?

The more these questions are answered by your pitch, the more the audience can hear what you're trying to say.

If you launch into the pitch too early, trying to cram in as many words as possible, you risk the audience staring blankly at you, wondering, "Why are you telling me this?" And while those questions are running around in the client's head, they are not listening to a word you're saying.

The audience will only pay attention to your pitch if they find you credible, and your credibility is built on the foundation of the first impression that you make. Your image makes up the majority of that first impression, with your first words filling in the gaps.

3.15 Opening Words

Here are some opening words for your pitch:

"Good morning"

How many different ways can you say those words, and what impression do they create about your pitch? How do they affect your credibility?

Practice with your colleagues, and ask for their feedback on:

What was their first impression?

What do they expect your pitch to be about?

How do they feel?

Do they want to hear more? Or less?

Consistency

For your pitch to have its maximum impact, it must be consistent. No personal small talk. No comparison of golf handicaps or football results. No enquiries about the wife, weekend or future holiday plans.

By all means, make small talk. Just make it relevant.

How many presentations have you sat through where the presenter made small talk while his or her colleague was getting the presentation ready?

Compare these two examples of how you might use this 'set up time'.

> "It will just take Fred a few minutes to set up before we get started. So, how was your weekend? Did you see the match? Oh, they're going to struggle this season, aren't they? I can't believe they sacked another manager! And with the world cup just around the... oh right we're all set. OK then. Ladies and gentlemen, I'd like to take this opportunity to..."

> "Just as we're setting up for our pitch to you today, I want to make sure we're going to cover everything you need to make an informed decision today, and also I'd like to check exactly how much time we have your undivided attention for, because I do appreciate you're busy and your schedules can change at short notice.... (waits for answer) so for the next 30 minutes I would like to take this opportunity to..."

Do you see the difference?

Can you feel how the first example breaks rapport, while the second builds it?

Opening

Let's look at some of the formats and structures that you can use in designing your pitch.

Signposting

What I'm going to be telling you about is...

The best known example of signposting is probably the old adage of "tell them what you're going to tell them, tell them and then tell them what you've told them".

You might briefly explain:

☑ Who you are

☑ Why are you pitching

☑ What's in it for the audience

☑ What you're going to talk about

☑ When the audience can ask questions

☑ Anything else you're going to include in your pitch

Signposting tells the audience what to expect, but that also removes an element of surprise. Some people don't like surprises, they like to know exactly what's happening. However, you can achieve both security and surprise with the next format.

The Outcome

By the end of this pitch...

If you state your outcome to the audience, everyone is clear about why they are there. An outcome must be under your control, so if you tell the audience that, by the end of your pitch, they will decide to buy your product, your outcome is not under your control and you'll probably irritate the audience too.

There's no harm in saying that you want the client's business. It's all too easy to assume that everyone knows it and instead act as if your role is to inform or educate the client. It's not.

By stating your outcome, you clearly imply your role and that lets the audience know the context within which you are building rapport, and that in turn makes it easier for you to gain rapport and develop the right working relationship.

An outcome is often preferable to a signpost, because it tells the audience where they will get to, even if the details of how they'll get there are kept as a surprise. An outcome has the advantage of *sounding* like a signpost while keeping your options open.

One Word

Pitching... That's the key to your success.

If a word sums up your entire pitch, or the problem that your proposal solves, then you can start with that word. Leave it hanging in the air for a moment before you continue, so that you don't lose its impact.

The Contradiction

Some people love this, some hate it.

Some of our customer say that ours is the best product they've ever used. I disagree.

Many people have told me that this is the best book on the art of pitching that they have ever read. I'm not so sure. That's why I've written another.

The contradiction begins with something familiar and turns it on its head, creating curiosity and sometimes encouraging the audience to side 'against' the presenter and therefore 'with' the pitch itself.

The Quotation

"A child's world is fresh and new and beautiful, full or wonder and excitement. It is our misfortune that for most of us that clear-eyed vision, that true instinct for what is beautiful and awe-inspiring, is dimmed and even lost before we reach adulthood[3]"

> "Ladies and gentlemen, for just a few minutes, I'm asking you to take a step back into your childhood now and watch with that clear eyed vision and that instinct for beauty as I introduce you to..."

---

3   Rachel Carson, The Sense of Wonder, 1965

The Dramatic Entrance

If you open your pitch with dramatic impact, you might certainly get the audience's attention, although you potentially create a high energy opening which you then have to work harder to maintain.

You can combine the principle of this opening with the Show and Tell. For example, you could relate the concept of hidden value to the idea of an antique vase that you found in your garage. You could use the vase as a metaphor for having something that you don't appreciate the true value of. To make a point about wasting an opportunity, 'accidentally' drop the vase and smash it. While the vase is worthless, the impact on the audience will be very real.

Imagine

Invite the audience to imagine themselves in a situation; either new or familiar.

"Imagine your first day at school..."

"Imagine a world where..."

Inviting the audience to imagine will tend to draw them into a more relaxed, receptive frame of mind. Just be sure to bring their attention firmly back to the room before you continue with your pitch.

Humour

If you want to introduce your pitch with humour, start easy. Use personal experiences, oddities, irony. The more personal your story, the more universally it is understood. Let the audience laugh at you, not at themselves.

Avoid telling jokes unless you're selling your services as a stand up comedian. This has nothing to do with your ability to tell jokes, it is because telling jokes and then moving into a business pitch breaks rapport. By opening with a joke, you establish your role as that of entertainer, not as business partner.

There is a place for levity and lightness but the best pitchers simply allow humour to flow from the situation if and when it is appropriate.

The Reference

If the company you're pitching to has a current, relevant news story or event, you can open your pitch with a reference to it.

The Promise

At the beginning of your pitch, make a prediction or promise. You can combine this with the previous tip by placing an answer in an envelope or box.

For example, you might promise that by the end of the pitch, a million births and deaths will have taken place in the room. In the box is a glass plate with bacteria on, to show the audience the power of your disinfectant product.

Show and Tell

You can use any object as a metaphor for the main message of your pitch. It might be something that literally represents your pitch, such as a product of demonstration model, or it might be a metaphor for the message of your pitch.

With this format, you can revisit your object throughout your pitch and use it in your closing too. It might even be something that you can leave at the front of the room when you leave, to serve as a reminder.

The Question

Instead of starting your pitch with a grand opening statement, why not start with a question?

Imagine you're at a conference. You meet with someone who you would dearly love to do business with. You say, "What one thing could we show you today that would make the whole conference worthwhile?"

Whatever they say, that's what you talk about. The entire pitch, centred around the one idea that will make the biggest difference to them.

You can stand on a street corner, shouting all day and before long, your pitch will become background noise. But ask someone a question and, even for a moment, they are hooked. They are instantly put into a receptive frame of mind. After that, it's up to you to put their attention to good use.

Closing the Loop

Many stories and films end with the same words as they open with. This looping neatly concludes a story and wraps everything together.

You could open your pitch with a powerful statement, such as a compelling statistic or a call to action and then repeat that statement as you conclude your pitch.

Starting and ending with the same thought provoking question can be very powerful. Here are some examples with the subject of their pitch:

Question	Subject
"What would you give to be able to correct one mistake in your life?"	A project to support disadvantaged teenagers
"How would it feel to save someone's life today?"	Funding for a health program
"What would an extra £10,000 in your business budget mean for you?"	An IT project that would lead to a cost saving of £10,000
"What would it take for you to make the right decision today?"	A general purpose question for any pitch that invites a decision

"How would you feel, knowing that you had changed the world today?"	Investment in a product that will save energy, cure an illness or markedly improve people's lives
"What would it mean to you to hear your name spoken in every house in the country"	An advertising campaign

Begin by posing the question. After leaving it to hang in the air for a few moments, move straight into your pitch. Do not refer back to your opening question or explain it in any way. At the end of your pitch, repeat the question. The content of your pitch has provided the answer, and the audience now knows what to do.

Here's an example script.

> "What would you give to be able to correct just one mistake in your life?
>
> My name is Stevie Smith and I run a project for teenagers who have been in trouble with the police. Typically, they struggled at school, dropped out and got into the wrong company. Through peer pressure, which I know we've all felt in one way or another, they end up making a mistake that they regret for the rest of their lives. I'm here to get your support, and through our project help these teenagers to put right that mistake and to make sure it doesn't take away their chance of a normal

life, the life that we can all too easily take for granted.

I'm asking for your sponsorship, your time, your brand or just your funding. Which you give is up to you, all are invaluable to us and to the people who are going to have a second chance in life, thanks to you.

After all, what would you give to be able to correct just one mistake in your life?"

The question takes on a different meaning as a result of what you say in the main body of the pitch, because the second question is now set in a new context.

The Old Curiosity Shop

Before you begin your pitch, place a mysterious object in plain sight of the audience. It might be a cardboard box, an envelope, an ornament, a toy or a picture.

For example. let's say you're pitching a business idea for a water saving device, so you place a bag of sugar on the lectern or table. At the end of your pitch, you illustrate the value of water by pointing out that every member of the audience's body is between 97% and 99% water, so if you took all of the water out of a human body, the sugar is the weight of what would remain. You can end by saying that we have to save water because, without water, this (the bag of sugar) is all that is left of us.

The Surprise

A variant of The Old Curiosity Shop can be used with a whiteboard, flip chart or even just a piece of paper.

Write some raw information such as numbers or simple facts. At the most impactful point in your pitch, reveal what the numbers or facts mean.

Let's say that you pitch a new product that helps children to learn to read.

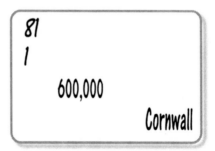

When you reach the relevant moments in your pitch, you can fill in the missing context:

> **81** % of the world's population is literate
>
> **1**% of the UK's population cannot read & write
>
> **That's 600,000 people in the UK!**
>
> **The entire population of Cornwall**

You can also see from this example that raw statistics are not very compelling. They're just numbers, and when you translate those numbers into something that the audience can relate to emotionally, your pitch takes on a whole new level of impact.

Of course, the other neat thing about this technique is that it saves you having to remember statistics, because they were in plain sight of the audience the whole time.

The key to this technique is leaving the 'teaser' in plain sight during your pitch, and filling in the context at the moment of greatest impact.

The Story

You can open your pitch with a story. It might be a well known story, a children's story, a story from your distant past or even a story about your journey to the client's offices.

Stories build rapport, lead the audience, influence their state, build empathy and can even influence the audience's beliefs.

The most important rule of thumb with a story is to never, ever explain what it means. Each member of the audience will have taken their own, personal meaning from the story, and if you tell them what the story means, you contradict that and break rapport.

Here's What I Want You To Do

In a pitch, it is a good idea to get the audience following instructions. You are there for your benefit, not as a servant of the client. You are entering into a mutually beneficial, equal business partnership.

Getting the client into the habit of doing things that you ask is very important in defining your relationship with them. The alternative is that you do everything they ask, ask them for nothing in return and when you ask for an order, they ask you for more discounts, more concessions and more time, because they have trained you to respond to them. At the very least, the playing field needs to be level.

The earlier you start asking the audience to follow your instructions, the more you are in control of yourself.

Timing

If you feel any nerves or anxiety at all, go for a soft opening such as a story. This allows you to relax into your pitch before you reach the pause and give your audience time to reflect on the story before moving into the main body of your pitch.

If you're nervous and your focus is on yourself, your sense of time will change. You might feel that you have been talking for a long time, only to find that you've rushed through your pitch in just five minutes. When you get drawn into a conversation, or if you're asked a difficult question, what seems like a few seconds to you can be minutes for the audience.

Pausing is an important way to add impact to your pitch. As a simple rule of thumb, a pause should be just long enough that you think it's too long.

If you feel that timing is an issue, remember a very simple tip. Keep an eye on the clock.

Never, Never, Ever

Apologise

For the start, the food, the weather, the confusion, the length of your pitch, the boredom, the time of day, for wasting the audience's time, for being alive.

"I'm sorry to take up your valuable time"

"Well don't then. Next!"

Make a Bad Joke

Never make a joke at the expense of someone in the audience, no matter who it is. It's unprofessional and it alienates you. Keep jokes like this for the pub.

Assume you Know the Audience

You're not like them, otherwise you would be sitting where they are.

Make the Audience Wait

Computer slides might reinforce your pitch but they are not your pitch. Product samples and demonstrations need to work right, first time. Videos need to play smoothly. **If in doubt, do without.**

Stick to the Script

The audience doesn't expect your pitch to be perfect. Very few clients want to buy something 'off the shelf', so if something isn't quite right, it's an opportunity for the client to be involved in its development.

Some presenters use small cards to remind themselves of their key points. There's no problem with doing this, although I would advise that you write as few words as possible on a card so that you don't have to spend time reading them, and you should number the cards in case they get mixed up.

An alternative is to draw a picture or icon on each card, as you may find you can take this in much more quickly without interrupting the flow of your pitch.

Follow Advice

You'll be plagued with friends and colleagues offering good advice about your pitch. Don't listen to what works for someone else, because that's what works for them.

Keep on working at what works for you

Secret Brief

Making a Connection

Make sure you have the audience's full attention before you say a word.

State

Your state shapes how you feel, how you perceive and how you behave.

Anchoring

Anchoring is a powerful method for accessing the state you want, and you can influence the audience's state too. On top of that, it's natural, organic and has zero calories.

Rapport

A connection between two or more people, an invisible communication medium and a powerful means of influence.

Group Rapport

The audience will act as a single entity, so make sure you're in control.

I'm Sorry, I'm Losing You

What do you do if you lose rapport? You need to decide before you pitch, not hope for the best and work it out as you go along.

Influence

Rapport is a two way street, so don't be so preoccupied with influencing the audience that you don't notice how much they're influencing you.

Territory

A good pitcher claims his or her territory and controls it for the duration of the pitch.

Making an Impression

The audience forms an impression of you in two to three seconds, and you have a high degree of control over that impression.

Non-Verbal Communication

Whilst some people debate the relative impact of verbal and non-verbal communication, we can at least agree that human beings communicate over multiple channels, and have very little conscious control over that process. Therefore, your true intentions leak out and in return, your audience broadcasts their reaction back to you.

Credibility

Before the audience can pay attention and put your pitch into context, you need to establish credibility. This will happen whether you like it or not, so it's best to take control and make the right impression.

Interruptions

Once you have decided how you want to handle interruptions, stick to it. If you want to let the audience take control of your pitch, you do more harm by making a half hearted effort. To be in control you have to risk being firm.

Consistency

Keeping the content and direction of your pitch builds rapport and prevents the uncomfortable "but seriously..." moment that usually follows an 'ice breaker'.

Opening

Planning the opening to your pitch needs much more careful thought than simply introducing yourself and launching in.

Your opening sets the stage, captures the audience's attention and connects through to the close of your pitch.

Timing

Jokes and dramatic openings rely on..... timing, so if you're nervous, avoid high impact openings.

And if all else fails, pause.

Never, Never, Ever

There are a few things to avoid doing during your pitch, apart from the obvious things like turning up in your pyjamas.

Never apologise, make bad jokes, make the audience wait or stick to the script.

And most of all, never take anyone's advice at face value.

Keep on working at what works for you

SECRET 4

DREAM
THE
DREAM

The Dream

Your pitch, your idea, was created in a dream world. In order for that dream to become a reality, you need to share that dream with the audience.

What I mean is that your pitch started with an idea. If you got in any way emotionally involved with that idea then you saw it, heard it, felt it and so on. You lived it. For a fleeting moment, that dream became your reality, and you have to draw the audience into that dream so that they can see, hear and feel it through their own perceptions and experiences.

When you begin your pitch, the audience has a preconception about what to expect. If you have followed my advice so far, you will have sent the audience an invitation, and in that invitation you will have influenced the audience's preconception about you and your pitch.

When you begin the main pitch, the part where you're speaking, you have to establish your dream as a shared reality. You need to invite the audience to suspend their beliefs and disbeliefs and be prepared to join you in that dream.

Don't Tell Us... Show Us

Your client doesn't want to know how wonderful you think your product or idea is. They want to find out for themselves.

If you tell the audience that your product is ground breaking, revolutionary or innovative then you aren't just putting words into their mouths, you're telling them what to think, and you don't like being told what to think, do you?

Telling the audience what to think breaks rapport.

What does the word 'innovative' mean to you? Is it good or bad? Every word has different meanings and implications for different people:

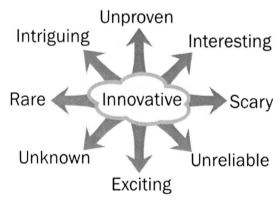

Words are metaphors, and whilst we have a broadly common understanding of language, our metaphors are sufficiently different that they can break rapport when used carelessly.

4.1 Synonyms

Try this experiment.

Ask 5 people around your office to give you a synonym (a word with a similar meaning) for the following words:

Professionalism

Innovative

Confusing

Complicated

Revolutionary

Excellence

Free

What did you discover?

What did the person's synonyms tell you about them?

What did their chosen words tell you about their experiences?

Did everyone come up with the same synonyms?

What happens if you repeat the experiment, asking for antonyms, words with the opposite meaning?

Does everyone agree on the opposites?

If people gave you different synonyms, they have different underlying metaphors, which means that they have different life experiences underpinning their understanding of those words.

Therefore, when you tell the audience that your product is innovative, each person accesses a different life experience in order to understand what you're talking about, and the group's involvement in your pitch breaks down.

Some will associate innovative with their brand new flat panel TV, others will associate it with a computer they bought ten years ago that never worked properly.

Innovation, reliability and quality are all irrelevant, really. What matters is the feeling that those words lead to – a feeling of desire and curiosity about the subject of your pitch.

When you are able to convey your dream, in all of its richness and vivid colour, into the minds of the audience and from that, let them draw their own conclusions as to how to describe it, they are selling themselves on their own idea. They have personalised it. They have mixed your words with their own life story. They have become part of your dream.

A Word on Sales... "Enthusiasm"

Sales is the transfer of enthusiasm from one individual to another.

Having enthusiasm means that you are emotionally engaged, and enthusiasm is made for sharing.

4.2 Enthusiasm

Take two pieces of paper.

On one, write the name of something that you are genuinely enthusiastic about. This is 'A'.

On the other, write the name of something that you are pitching. This is 'B'.

Stand in front of a clear desk or table and place them wherever makes the most sense for you.

Think about each one in turn; what it involves, what it represents and so on.

Then, pick up the two pieces of paper and put 'B' where 'A' was.

Keep 'A' out of sight and concentrate on 'B'.

How does that feel different?

What insights did you gain into why you feel the way that you do about 'B'?

How else could you use this?

Enthusiasm is just one of countless emotions that you are capable of experiencing.

What makes an emotional response? In particular, when you recall a memory, how do you know how to feel? Think of something that gives you that sinking feeling, and then think of something that makes you feel warm and fuzzy. How do you know the difference?

Here's the interesting thing: for many people, happy memories are big, bright and colourful. Unhappy memories tend to be small and dark. Why is this interesting? Think of the implications. It turns out that the emotional label on a memory is not directly related to the content of the memory – it's related to the structure of it. For example, you could watch the same film on a small black and white screen, on a large colour screen, at the cinema or even performed 'live' at the theatre. How you feel about the story changes with its presentation.

Good memories are big, bright, colourful, close, sharp, **vivid** and *moving*.

Bad memories are small, dim, dull, far away, fuzzy and still.

Every experience that you have ever had arrived through your senses, so everything you have ever seen has taken up your entire field of view and every sound has been as clear as what you are hearing now. So when you think of a time when you felt hurt or disappointed, why does it seem different?

Your brain codes the meaning of a memory through these qualities, not within the content itself, so the events don't change, but your perception of them can. What happens to you is separate from what it means to you and what you do about it.

Does this sound familiar? Think back to Secret Three where we talked about non-verbal communication. The tonal and visual elements of communication do not, for the most part, carry a message of their own, instead they modify the verbal message.

So while you may not have noticed before that bad memories tend to be small, dark and distant, now that you have noticed, you might want to do something about it.

4.3 The Structure of Memories

Try this at home: ask someone to remember a time when they experienced a particular emotional state – anything will do, although strong states are easier to work with.

Go through each of the qualities listed above and find out how your partner structures their memory. Then have them pick a different state and go through the process again, noticing which qualities have changed.

Here are some states that you can try this with:

Surprised **Confused** **Anxious**

Smug **Curious** **Argumentative**

Worried **Relieved** **Enthusiastic**

Compare how they structure a memory differently than you do, for a given state. For example, with a 'surprised' memory, your picture might be large, theirs might be small. Do you notice a connection between the differences and how they feel about the state or event?

Let's say for example that 'enthusiastic' had a picture above eye level, at about arms length, bright and colourful, whilst 'worried' had a picture down on the floor, over to the left, dark and colourless.

What if we take the picture of 'worried', move it, turn up the brightness and colour, would it change? Try it for yourself and see the difference.

Think of something in the future that you are not looking forward to. Can you change the qualities of the thought to change your response, so that you actually feel more motivated? Yes you can, very easily. It's even easier to change responses for future events because they haven't happened yet.

If you do want to use computer slides, and knowing what you know now about the correlation between emotional states and visual qualities, how will you design your slides differently?

Changing States

If you look at your client's desk, where do they put things that they really don't want to deal with, like their tax return or some HR paperwork?

Where do they put important items, such as urgent reports?

And where do they put things that are personally valuable to them, such as their family photos?

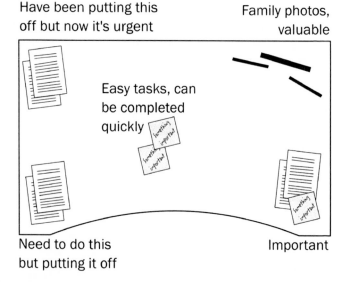

Have been putting this off but now it's urgent

Family photos, valuable

Easy tasks, can be completed quickly

Need to do this but putting it off

Important

Let's translate their physical workspace into an analogous mental workspace.

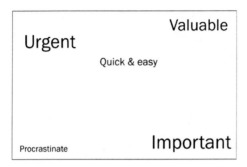

Finally, let's put that mental workspace onto a presentation slide:

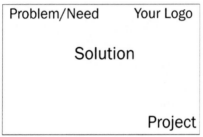

And a page of a proposal:

In this example, the 'problem' or 'need' would be a name or symbol for the business problem that the client is trying to solve and the 'project' is a name or symbol for what you are proposing. Your actual solution, the specific thing that the client's decision is based on, is in their 'quick and easy' space, which makes it less likely for them to put it off by moving it into their 'procrastinate' space.

Here's an example running order for your slides.

First, current situation, smaller and darker.

Current Situation

Next, the specific problem that the current situation presents. Slightly bigger to create tension.

Problem

Next, your solution, big and bright to release that tension.

Your Solution

Next, alternative options, smaller and darker. Logically, this creates balance and impartiality. Emotionally, it creates tension again, because you have taken away the bright, happy slide.

Alternative Options

Next, your solution again, big and bright, to release that tension.

Your Solution

Finally, your solution again, bigger and brighter to end on an emotional high.

Your Solution

If a number of potential suppliers are pitching to the client, then any one of them could, on paper, give the client what they want. Why shouldn't that be you? And why would you leave that outcome to chance?

And, if you're sufficiently interested in your own success to be reading this, the chances are that your competitors are too. Which of you is going to gain the advantage by putting this into practice?

Stealing the Space

A lectern is both a physical barrier and a reminder of all the poor pitches that have come before you, so it's twice as important to step out and face your audience.

When you walk into the client's meeting room, the room layout will tell you where every past presenter has stood. The chairs and table, the whiteboard, the flip charts, even the door and windows will tell you where you should stand for maximum influence.

Choosing the location that you want to pitch from is an important part of claiming your territory, and it is all part of being in control of how you feel, and how you feel directly influences how the audience feels and therefore the outcome of your pitch.

Fun

70.9% of corporate buyers said that they would switch suppliers on the basis that the new supplier was more fun[4].

---

4   According to a book that I read on guerilla marketing.

I'm not suggesting you take your client to the fun fair and win them a goldfish, I'm suggesting that every interaction with them has to be upbeat, optimistic, positive and recognise that you are in this together. A problem shared is a problem solved.

Remember, a client is for life, not just for Christmas

The Future's Bright

The technique of mental rehearsal can equally be used with the client to help them mentally rehearse their future working relationship with you.

The future's bright, so you need to make it literally big, bright and colourful. I'm not talking about the inflated claims that some advertisers make, which simply make the client suspicious and cynical. Set the client's expectations so that you can meet them. Not exceed them. Meet them.

Do not claim that:

☒ You are world class or unique – everyone is!

☒ Your tech support staff have great interpersonal skills – that's not why you hired them!

☒ Your sales team will be there right the way through the process – that's not what you pay them to do!

☒ Your CEO loves receiving calls about any problems, day or night – he has a company to run!

What I'm talking about is a realistic expectation of the working relationship, communicated in a way that is vivid and compelling.

Here's a very simple, practical way to do this.

4.4 Big and Bright

Think about a client who you will be pitching to for new business.

Imagine the working relationship with them.

Is the picture you see big or small? Bright or dark? Near or far? Is it a movie or a still photograph? Is it colourful or grey?

Be aware of the qualities of the image and notice any important information that this gives you, for example, if the picture is small and dark, are you dreading working with the client?

However the picture looked to begin with, make it big, bright, colourful, close and moving.

If you see things in the picture that you don't think are realistic, change them.

Now describe the picture to a friend or colleague.

Ask your friend or colleague to tell you how they feel about the future working relationship that you have just described to them. Ask them what their impression is; did you seem optimistic about the future? Do they feel optimistic? What questions do they have about it?

When you describe your big, bright, colourful, vivid mental image of your working relationship with the client, you don't need to say that it's big, bright and colourful. It will be written all over your face. It will shine through in your voice tone. Your hands will be painting a gigantic, vivid poster.

4.5 Opportunities

Imagine that you sell computers. You win an order from a new client, but the technical department tell you that the model of computer that the client has ordered has just been superseded by a higher spec model. You call the client to tell them. Do you say:

A. Great news! I've got an even better deal for you! I spoke to my boss and twisted his arm to let you have a higher 'spec' for the same price!

B. Another client just cancelled an order for a higher spec model than the one you've ordered. Normally we would return them to the manufacturer, but if you bought a year's maintenance, I could let you have them for the same price as the ones you've ordered.

C. Just before I put the order through, I want to check the details. Do you know that you can get a higher spec model, which would probably give you another couple of years' lifespan, for only a little more?

If you answered A then you'll do anything to please. If you're in sales, you probably run around a lot more than you need to, and if you manage to hit your sales target at all, it feels like a struggle.

If you answered B then you're doing OK, you see the opportunity. Unfortunately, if the client says "no, thanks" you're left in the awkward position of having to supply the higher spec anyway, and the client will realise that you tried to use it to your advantage.

If you answered C, you are trying to open the conversation again. When the client says that, unfortunately, their budget is fixed, you can offer the client the same price in return for something else that is of value.

Good sales people only exceed the client's expectation when that is worth something to the client and can therefore be traded. If all it's worth is to make the client happy, a good sales person remembers that the client is already happy, otherwise they wouldn't be buying from you. They don't need to be any happier.

I Dreamed a Dream

Everything that you can see around you began as a dream, an idea in someone's mind.

How you convey your dream into your client's mind determines how and when it becomes a reality.

This Secret has dealt with how you convey not information but meaning in your pitch, and the meaning is the basis upon which your audience will make a decision.

We are meaning making machines; we assess huge volumes of sensory data, most of it outside of our awareness, and reach an instant conclusion. When we act on that conclusion, we do so with a degree of certainty.

When the meaning and message of your pitch align with your client's certainty, you know you are heading in the right direction.

Secret Brief

The Dream

Your pitch began as a dream, an idea. Your pitch draws the audience into that dream and makes it real.

Don't Tell Us What to Think... Show Us

Don't tell the audience what to think about your pitch because this breaks rapport. Use concepts and metaphors to paint a picture and allow the audience to draw their own conclusions.

A Word on Sales... "Enthusiasm"

Sales is the transfer of enthusiasm from one individual to another, and enthusiasm is infectious. In fact, any strong state is infectious.

Changing States

Not only are states infectious, they each have their own unique characteristics and language that can be used to change them.

Once you have learned to influence and change states, you can borrow them from other people too.

Journey

A pitch is an emotional journey, leading the audience through ups and downs, highs and lows to an action packed ending.

Fun

70.9% of corporate buyers said that they would switch suppliers on the basis that the new supplier was more fun.

The Future's Bright

A big, bright, colourful, vivid future makes almost anything worth having.

I Dreamed a Dream

Everything around you began as an idea, and someone had to pitch those ideas in order to make them a reality.

Sales is the transfer of enthusiasm from one individual to another

SECRET 5

MIND

YOUR

LANGUAGE

The Language of Pitching

We've talked about conveying the meaning of your pitch, so now it's time to communicate the information that the audience needs to support that meaning.

Once you open your mouth to speak, you are, of course, using language to communicate ideas.

As we saw in Secret Four, Dream The Dream, words are a fairly sparse means of communicating rich and vivid information, and so the listener will be filling in a lot of gaps in order to make sense of what you say. Most of those gaps will be filled with your non-verbal communication, and the rest will be filled with the client's preconceptions.

They say that you cannot not communicate, and once you have made an initial connection with someone, you're forever communicating with them. Have you ever jumped to a conclusion when someone didn't call you as promised? They communicated with you by doing absolutely nothing.

Because it's practically impossible to fully describe anything in language alone, we rely on the recipient of our communication to have some knowledge to build upon.

Features and Benefits

Sales people most often say, "Here's the feature, which means that you get this benefit".

It's the wrong way round.

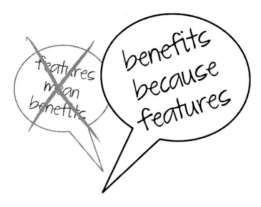

By the time you're half way through describing the feature, the audience is already thinking about the benefit. When you finally get round to the benefit, it will be different to what they had in mind. Even the most subtle difference will break rapport.

Compare these two examples:

"This book contains the seven secrets of perfect pitches which means that you can read it quickly and easily"

"This book gives you everything you need to know because it contains all seven secrets of perfect pitches."

With "Feature Means Benefit", the audience has already imagined a benefit by the time you have finished describing the feature, and because that will be different to how you describe the benefit, the result is a subtle disagreement which breaks rapport.

With "Benefit Because Feature", the audience accepts the benefit first as something worth having and is then waiting to find out how that benefit can be achieved.

5.1 Features and Benefits

Think of your own product, or pick something that's in front of you at the moment.

Get a piece of paper and write out six features that it has. Then write out the six benefits of those features.

Finally, ask two other people what they think the benefits of those features might be and write those down too.

Make sure you write down exactly the words that each person uses – that's the key to why this works. It's important that you discover for yourself that different people will interpret the features differently.

Yes, there will be many common themes in the benefits that your colleagues suggest, yet it's the differences that are most valuable, because they contain the keys to making your pitch stand head and shoulders above your competitors'.

WIIFM?

There are differences in the benefits that people attribute to a product's features because each person is listening through their own 'WIIFM?' filter.

This special filter allows you to ask "What's In It For Me?" whenever you're presented with a fact or decision. You might also experience this as the "So What?" filter, the "Why Should I Care?" filter and the "Don't Tell Me What To Think" filter.

Our 'WIIFM?' filter evaluates incoming information to judge it against our own beliefs and perception of the world. It protects us from accepting other people's beliefs too readily. It prevents us from accepting new information too.

When you begin to notice how the audience interprets the features of your product, you will realise just how much you can discover about their inner world; their motivations, interests, fears and, most importantly, their buying criteria.

Firstly, you can make sure that the people you're pitching to are in as receptive a state as possible before you begin. We talked about ways that you can do this in the Secret Two.

Receptive States

☑ Use every opportunity to communicate with the audience prior to the presentation

☑ Frame the presentation - let the audience know what to do

☑ Answer the audience's unspoken questions

☑ Build rapport with the audience

Secondly, you can use the two simple, everyday forms of communication which will bypass the 'WIIFM?' filter completely.

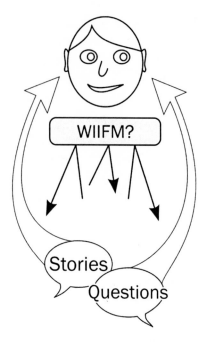

Questions

"Telling is not selling"

Questions are a very powerful way to convey new concepts because they build on the what the audience already knows. BA question bypasses the listener's critical 'WIIFM?' filter. However, in order for the listener to make sense of the question, they must accept whatever it presupposes.

For example, what have you found to be the most valuable part of this book for you?

This question presupposes that the book has more than one valuable part, that you find it valuable and that you have already realised that value.

We hear questions when:

☑ The speaker's voice pitch rises through a sentence

☑ A sentence starts with a word such as why, when, where, how, what, which, who, if, is, could, would, will, won't, might, may, can, etc.

☑ A statement ends with a tag question, such as couldn't it, don't they, do we, can it, etc.

Asking questions about your presentation subject can be a very effective way to ensure the audience has all the information they need to make an informed decision.

5.2 Questions

Can you deliver the opening part of your pitch using only questions?

What effect would that have?

What questions would you ask?

Could you practice that right now?

Stories

Human beings communicate with each other in a narrative. We don't communicate using factual statements alone; they are linked by a narrative, which includes characters – who did what to who – and a sequence in time, so that we can recreate the situation mentally. Imagination is a close substitute for the real thing[5], and stories are the gateway to the fundamental process of human learning.

---

5   Even John Lennon said, "Reality leaves a lot to the imagination".

As one person is talking, anyone listening is translating their words back into the original sensory experience. Of course, they can't translate it into exactly the original, so they are substituting their own experiences and references in order to make sense of it. The person listening to the story puts themselves in it. As they empathise, they 'get the message'.

"I get the message"

What does this mean for you?

For a start, it means that the more narrative you use, the easier you are to listen to.

Secondly, it means that the richer your narrative, the more accurate are the pictures you create in your audience's mind.

Narrative communication – storytelling - is vital, it's natural, and you already have a lot of experience in using it:

☑ Anecdotes

☑ Case studies

☑ Reports

☑ Any description of an event

5.3 Stories

Set aside some time at work, perhaps ten minutes, to listen to stories. Try not to get drawn into them, instead just sit back and observe. Monday morning is an ideal time to do this because you can sit at your desk, pretending to read a document, listening to your colleagues' stories of their weekend antics.

Pay attention to the stories and, in particular, notice what images pop into your mind as you listen. Notice how the stories engage you, even if you have no specific interest in them. Why do you think this is?

The Elevator Pitch

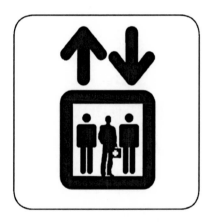

Never, never ever try to cram your pitch into three minutes, or into any length of time for that matter.

Instead, focus on how that three minutes is the trailer for the movie, the hook that leaves them saying "Call me" instead of "erm.. well it was nice meeting you".

You might even practice your elevator pitch and use it as the introduction to your main pitch, just like a newspaper headline gives you a reason and motivation to read the full story.

This is such a vital skill for the professional presenter, not only for the chance meeting in the elevator but in any pitching situation, because you can generally guarantee that you won't have the amount of time that you thought you were going to have.

Remember, a pitch is not a one way communication. Given an hour or ten minutes or even one minute, your focus must not be on cramming as much information into the audience as possible, because they can't take it all in anyway.

Sorry, we're a bit pushed for time.

Can you do your pitch in ten minutes?

When you walk in the door expecting an hour, or half an hour, or whatever has been agreed, you should fully expect that to change and have a plan in place to take full advantage of the opportunity.

Here is a checklist that you can use to prepare for any last minute schedule changes.

> **Preparation**
>
> ☑ What is your outcome for your pitch?
>
> ☑ What do you want the audience to do?
>
> ☑ What is the most important thing to get across?
>
> ☑ How will you achieve that in the time allowed?
>
> ☑ How will you achieve that in half that time?
>
> ☑ How will you achieve that in five minutes?
>
> ☑ How will you achieve that in one minute?

You Know How...

Think about stand up comedians who start a routine with "You know how..."

Yes! I know exactly how! Oh my God, that happened to me! I have hairs in my plug hole! My kettle makes a noise like that! I wear shoes too!

Yes, we all have those same experiences. They're just not particularly funny until we all sit in a big room, get drunk and listen to someone else talk about them. We all like to share in the social bonding experience of agreeing that the government is corrupt and that our kitchen utensils are trying to kill us.

The comedian builds a routine on those experiences.

You can build your pitch on them.

State the Obvious

Often, presenters fear insulting the audience's intelligence, so they avoid stating the obvious.

In fact, stating the obvious is important in developing rapport as it draws the audience into your world.

For example, if you thank the audience at the beginning of your pitch, you can either say, "Thank you for coming", or you can say, "Thank you for your time, I know you have travelled to be here".

The second version makes a statement which everyone can agree with, unless they live in the presentation room. Its effect is a subtle alignment of rapport, and it is a very important step in gaining a high level of group rapport for your pitch.

You can begin your pitch with universal truths, and you can also wrap those truths in questions.

"Have you wondered why there aren't more good books on the subject of pitching?"

When you're pitching, you are inviting the audience to suspend their beliefs and join you in your imaginary world.

Stating the obvious, or stating universal truths, is an excellent way to build rapport.

Phrases such as, "It seems obvious, yet...", or, "Many people find that...", or, "You might already know that..." soften the statement, making it more acceptable.

The danger area is where something seems obvious, so you stress, "obviously...", or "we all know that...", as if anyone who doesn't is an idiot.

Even if it's something that you think everyone in the audience should know, you can guarantee that at least one person doesn't, or at least thinks that they don't.

To build rapport at the start of your pitch, you might consider using statements like these:

☑ I appreciate you have all made the time to be here

☑ I know you've all travelled to be here

☑ It's good to see you all here today

☑ I know some people couldn't be here today

☑ Now that you're all sitting down...

☑ There is water on the table for you

☑ I'm here today to...

Alternatively, you can use questions:

☑ Do you want to get some water before I begin?

☑ Are you sitting comfortably?

☑ Can you hear me clearly?

☑ Can you see me OK if I stand here?

☑ Can you see the screen clearly?

☑ Are you ready for me to begin?

☑ Can I check some points before I begin?

Getting a Feel For Language

How many different ways do you hear people say, "I understand"? Do these sound familiar?

I get it	I can grasp that
I see	That sounds right
I hear you	I'm with you
That's crystal clear	I dig
That's clear as a bell	Looks great
Sounds good to me	I can get my head round it
That feels right	You're on my wavelength

When you hear these, you probably translate them all into a confirmation of understanding, rather than paying attention to the particular words used.

In fact, the specific words that a person uses tell us whether they are primarily thinking in images, sounds or feelings.

Here are some of those phrases again, with their associated sensory system:

I get it	Feel
I see	See
I hear you	Hear
That's crystal clear	See or Hear
That's clear as a bell	Hear
That sounds right	Hear
I'm with you	Feel
Looks great	See

The words that someone uses gives you clues about how they are thinking, and this is valuable both in gaining rapport and in influencing their thoughts.

Here are some more sensory words that you can use to make your pitch even more vivid and compelling.

Visual

See	Vision	Sharp
Picture	Outlook	Background
Look	Bright	Shine
Watch	Clear	Reflect
Perspective	Focus	Magnify

Auditory (Tonal)

Listen	Quiet	Whistle
Hear	Amplify	Whine
Sound	Tell	Roar
Noise	Resonate	Silent
Loud	Clear	Tone

Auditory (Verbal)

Say	Think	Ask
Speak	Reason	Instruct
Tell	Know	Read
Question	Logical	Dialogue
Chatter	Interpret	Translate

Kinaesthetic

Feel	Push	Down
Touch	Embrace	Ache
Grab	Warm	Gut
Hold	Cold	Queasy
Contact	Sinking	Shaky

Back in Secret Three, we were talking about eye movements and how they relate to a person's thought processes. In fact, these sensory thought processes are evident in many more ways, one of which is a person's language.

5.4 Sensory Language

When you next watch the news on TV, or listen to it on the radio, pay attention to the unscripted interviews. Listen out for people using these words. Notice how their language comes alive with a new depth and meaning as you realise how literal these words are, and how the person is describing their inner experience.

Of course, you can try this with real people too, it's just that people on TV don't seem to mind as much when you stare at them.

Make a note of your colleagues' preferences and begin to respond to them using words that match their preference. Notice the response you get.

Finally, try deliberately mismatching. For example, if someone has a strong visual preference, use kinaesthetic words and notice what happens.

You might be wondering how to use this.

Let's say that you meet a client and he says, "Look, I'm interested in seeing what we could work on together. I think you've got an interesting perspective on our business problems and I think you can help bring some focus to what we're working on. Send me a proposal and we'll look it over."

Well, that's screaming 'visual' language, isn't it? And that tells you how to phrase your response so that it makes the right connection.

Vaguely Specific

Politicians and other public communicators use a form of language which is vague, but which seems oddly specific when you first hear it.

"People will understand that the solutions to these kinds of problems are to be found not in the past but in the future, and everyone will appreciate what a difficult task this can be. You can also be certain that the government you have now is in a far better position than any other to tackle these problems and to resolve them in a way that is economical, effective and respectful to the local community."

Does that sound familiar? Perhaps you remember hearing that before? Actually, I just made it up.

Expert pitchers, politicians, leaders and storytellers can communicate directly with every listener or reader in a very personal and individual way.

You've no doubt heard excellent public speakers using this technique, perhaps using phrases such as:

☑ Times are changing

☑ Our industry has changed beyond recognition

☑ The market is certainly very different

☑ People need to feel they can rely on us

☑ I know that you will agree when I say...

☑ I've listened to what you've told me...

How can you be a little more vague? Particularly at the outset of your pitch, this is an excellent way to gain rapport. And people really enjoy feeling in rapport, don't they?

Presuppositions

Presuppositions are the components of the sentence which must be held true in order for the sentence to be grammatically correct.

Words can be vague, and often the only way to grasp the intended meaning is through context. When we hear language, we process all possible meanings and hold them temporarily until one stands out by fitting the context of the information.

Presuppositions are a very powerful influence tool.

☑ It will be easier when he's gone

☑ When are you leaving?

☑ Who are you going to fire next?

☑ You always enjoy pitching once you've started

☑ Your colleagues will be so pleased that you told them to buy this book

5.5 Presuppositions

Probably the best way to practice using these linguistic tools is:

1. Notice how other people use them naturally
2. Catch yourself using them naturally
3. Notice how they reveal underlying beliefs
4. Begin to use them purposefully
5. Practice when you're not pitching
6. Incorporate them into your pitches

Modal Operators

How do you feel about these statements?

☑ I am going to get ready for my pitch

☑ I could get ready for my pitch

☑ I will get ready for my pitch

☑ I ought to get ready for my pitch

☑ I need to get ready for my pitch

☑ I should get ready for my pitch

☑ I'll try to get ready for my pitch

☑ I must get ready for my pitch

The differences between these examples may be subtle, so just take a moment to go back and picture what each example brings to mind for you. Compare the differences between each example.

It's easy to say, "It's just words", but remember that words are a superficial symptom of our inner emotional state. Words give away secrets that we would rather keep to ourselves.

Think about something that you do easily. What do you say to yourself as you think about it?

☑ Can

☑ Will

☑ Want

☑ Am

☑ Need

Now think about something that you're really good at almost getting round to. Something that needs doing, but you really don't want to do it, so you always find a way to avoid it. What do you say to yourself as you think about it?

☑ Ought

☑ Should

☑ Must

☑ Could

☑ Try

Do you notice a pattern here?

5.6 Motivation

Take something that you need to do, such as some paperwork. Pay attention to how you talk to yourself about it. If, for example, you say, "I really ought to do that today" then actively change the words. Say out loud, "I am going to do that today".

Of course, you haven't done it yet, it is in the future and is therefore still an uncertainty. We can make the effect even more powerful by shifting it into the past:

"By the end of the day I will have done that"

Now we have the problem that "the end of the day" is not very specific. Which day? When exactly does it end? We can go one better:

"By the time I walk out of the door to go home today, I will have done that"

Stand up. Look up. Take a deep breath. Smile. Think about something you really love doing and really enjoy. Now say in a confident, musical voice:

"By the time I walk out of the door to go home today, I will have done that"

Now take something that you know you should do less of.

Sit down. Look down. Now say in a nervous, flat voice:

"I really ought to do that soon"

What do you notice about how you're thinking about these two tasks or activities?

This is a verbal version of the exercises that you completed in Secret Four where you swapped pieces of paper around and changed the qualities of your memories.

Listen carefully to the words that someone uses when they talk about something they enjoy doing. Then make sure you use those exact words back to them when you talk about what you want them to do.

Notice the words the other person uses, and use their words. Yours might make sense to them, or they might have the opposite effect. For example, 'must' motivates some people and stops others because it implies rules, and some people automatically follow rules whereas others automatically question them, so always pay attention to the person you want to develop a relationship with.

Commands

A command is an instruction. If pitching was as easy as just telling the client to buy from you, you wouldn't need my help.

Therefore, we need ways to get the message across which are less confrontational than a command whilst more powerful than a tentative suggestion.

Direct Commands

Often, the simplest way to get someone to do something is to tell them to do it.

"Please let me have your attention for a moment while I make an important announcement"

Direct commands are easily intercepted by a 'WIIFM?' filter. You can respond with "erm... no thanks". Or worse still, "Why should I?"

There are other ways to give someone a command, none of which is guaranteed to work, and all of them leave control with the client. You will not be able to command someone against their will, but when all other things are equal, these methods can tip the balance in your favour. For example, if the client is weighing up two proposals, and they just can't choose between them, subtle methods such as these can make a significant difference to the outcome.

The client might say, "Either of the two proposals gave us what we need, and in the end we just felt that your pitch was stronger. I can't put my finger on why, call it intuition."

Embedded Commands

An embedded command is an instruction embedded within a longer language structure. The simplest form is to embed "Enjoy my pitch" into "I hope that you enjoy my pitch".

A more complex form is, "I was a bit nervous this morning but my friend told me to just *relax and enjoy my pitch*, so I'll do my best".[6]

You might mark a command with a slight change in emphasis or a pause before or after the command.

The more subtle the better. You should probably practice this on your friends before you use it in a pitch. It's a good idea to tell your friends that you're doing it so that they can give you feedback.

---

6   Because a third party is saying the command, this also takes on the form of a story, making it more influential

Negative Commands

In the real world, there are no zeroes, negatives or opposites; things can only exist.

☑ Don't tell all your friends to buy The Pitching Bible

☑ Tell none of your friends to buy The Pitching Bible

☑ Tell your friends to buy a book, but not The Pitching Bible

All of these statements require you to tell your friends to buy The Pitching Bible, otherwise the negation doesn't make sense. But don't try this in your pitches, you never know what might happen.

Now

5.7 Where is Now?

Imagine that you can see the flow of time as a visible line connecting past, present and future.

Where is the past? Behind you, to the side or somewhere else?

Where is the future? Front? Side? Somewhere else?

Where is now? Inside? Outside?

How big is now? (Indicate with your hands)

How long is now? (Seconds, minutes, hours etc.)

Ask your friends, colleagues and family to answer these questions and note how they 'see' time.

Think about the differences between you and other people.

Do these differences explain any confusion or conflict that you have ever experienced relating to time, such as deadlines, priorities or a sense of urgency?

Some of us see time as a series of impending deadlines, others see it as a range of possible paths ahead of us. And each of us has a different interpretation of the duration of "now".

An important aspect of time is expectation. Generally, people don't mind if something takes you an hour, or a week, just as long as they can plan in advance. If you say that you'll get something done 'right away' and it takes you until tomorrow, have you met the expectation that you set?

5.8 How Soon is Soon?

What period of time do these words imply to you?

Now	Soon	A moment
Currently	Recently	Right away
Imminent	ASAP	Immediate
Not long	A minute	Eventually
Not long ago	Ages	A while
A bit	Forever	A tick
Five minutes	A second	Back then

Ask your friends, family and colleagues to answer the questions too. What differences do you notice? How is that interesting?

What will you do differently when someone says they'll call you back "in five minutes" or when a client says they will review your proposal, "soon"?

Perhaps you might ask for a specific date and time?

Consider a decision that you need to make. How do you feel differently about the following?

☑ You need to decide soon

☑ You need to decide imminently

☑ You need to decide at some point

☑ You need to decide right away

☑ You need to decide now

Think about the conversations you had with people while you were trying out exercises 5.7 and 5.8. When you understand what your client means by 'now', you can design your slides, write your proposal and present your pitch so that the client feels an inexplicable sense of urgency around making a decision. And, after all, if your pitch is important enough for them to spend time paying attention to you, it's important enough to act upon right away, isn't it? If something's important, why wait?

Put it in Writing

With a written pitch, you're not in control of the reader's attention, so you have to get your message across as quickly and succinctly as possible.

The usual way to do this is to put the summary first, perhaps as an 'executive summary' or a 'management summary', however it should be aimed at any reader, because anyone who takes the time to read your proposal is a potential decision maker or influencer.

A news story starts with a headline, and it is often said that the purpose of the headline is to make you want to read the story. This isn't strictly true:

The purpose of a headline is to make it easy for you to decide whether to read further or not

The importance of this is that the writer of the headline isn't trying to con the reader into reading the article, they're trying to influence who reads the article. The writer only wants people who are really interested in the article to read further.

Fantastic headline appeals to many

Thousands of people were led to read a news story yesterday and then found it boring and not at all related to their interests.

Their conclusion was that the whole magazine was boring and not relevant for them.

Selective headline appeals to few

Hundreds of people read a news story yesterday and found it very relevant.

Eye witnesses said that many other readers saw the headline and then turned the page to another article which was better suited to their needs.

All of the readers reported that the magazine was very interesting and relevant.

Headline

Your proposal needs a short, informative title such as "Proposal for Investment in a New TV Channel".

Remember, if you use words like 'groundbreaking' or 'opportunity', you're likely to make the reader think, "I'll be the judge of that!", which alienates them.

After the title, the next thing that the reader sees is the summary, which answers the question, "Why am I reading this?"

The summary should be between half a page and a page in length and should address the main points of the proposal.

The summary needs to address all of the decision maker's primary decision criteria and leave them asking the question that will be answered by the rest of the proposal.

That question is, "but *how*?"

Six Questions

Your proposal needs to answer, in detail, the questions that the reader will have before they can make a decision.

Why

What is the reason for the proposal?

Are you addressing an identified business need, or is this a speculative proposal?

Why should the reader consider your proposal?

Why should the reader read more?

What

What are you proposing?

What are you asking for?

What are you offering in return?

What is your solution to the reader's business problem?

What will your proposal do for the reader?

How

How does your solution address the reader's needs?

How does your solution work?

Where

Where is the solution to be delivered?

When

When can the solution be delivered?

When does the client need to make a decision?

When does the client need to place an order?

Who

Who will be delivering the solution?

What does the client need to know about you and your company?

Call to Action

Your proposal needs to tell the reader what to do next.

The next step might be a meeting, an appointment with a designer, the supply of information or an order form. Remember, if you're not asking for something then you're not writing a proposal.

Purpose

A written proposal should not be a word longer than is necessary to get the reader to make a decision.

Speak Your Mind

Your true feelings and intentions show up in your language, whether you like it or not. When you feel half hearted about something you try, and maybe, and should and ought.

Information never motivated anyone. Meaning is the reason why we do what we do, and your audience's search for meaning must be the start of your pitch, not the end of it.

Don't waste time trying to get every word right. Use the principles in this Secret, and this book, to get your goals and intentions right, and practice some of these linguistic tools to give your pitch the extra edge. If you try to follow a script that isn't coming from your heart, your audience will most definitely know about it.

By all means, mind your language, as long as you also remember to speak your mind.

Secret Brief

The Language of Pitching

Words are a sparse way to communicate your rich, vivid ideas into the client's mind. However, it's rather limiting to pitch without them. You need to understand how to use them to your fullest advantage.

Features and Benefits

Remember, it's benefits because features. Convey meaning first, then the information to support it.

WIIFM?

Get past the audience's 'WIIFM?' filter before they can listen to you

Questions

Questions don't convey information, do they?

Questions bypass the 'WIIFM?' filter and encourage interactivity.

Stories

I once met a man who told stories during his pitches, and they engaged and enthralled the audience like nothing else I've seen.

The Elevator Pitch

The Elevator Pitch is a trailer for the real thing. Don't try to cram everything into as short a time as possible, use any brief opportunity to move to the next stage; a pitch, not a purchase.

You Know How...

Familiar experiences draw people together and the rules of improvisation help to build rapport. Comedians use these techniques to get laughs. You can use them to win your pitch.

Getting a Feel for Language

Subtleties of language reveal how a person prefers to think. If you present information in their preferred way, you make it easier for them to understand.

Vaguely Specific

Hypnotists often have a bad image, especially where influence and persuasion are concerned. However, they do know a thing or two about communication, and there are a few tips that we can learn from them.

Commands

Often, the easiest way to get someone to do something is to tell them to do it. And if that doesn't work, just ask nicely.

Now

What do you want? And when do you want it?

Now is a rather vague period of time, and it's worth understanding what it really means.

Put it in Writing

Follow the same principles for a written pitch as you would for a face to face pitch.

Speak Your Mind

Whilst language is definitely important, don't try to script every word. Know what your outcome is, understand your pitch inside out and speak from your heart.

SECRET 6
SAY IT
AGAIN
SAM

Make it Memorable

Apparently, Humphrey Bogart never actually said, "Play it again, Sam" in the film Casablanca. Similarly, Captain Kirk never actually said, "Beam me up, Scotty". And we don't like watching home videos because nostalgia is so much better than the real thing.

No matter how well we think we remember an event, we can always get a contradictory account from someone else who was there. Since each person interprets the event through their own senses, and each person's senses are filtered according to their own experiences, beliefs and expectations, we shouldn't be surprised when each person's memory of the event is different.

Therefore, one of the things that excellent pitchers do is to make sure that their message is getting across, exactly as they intended it to.

No doubt you have heard (perhaps earlier in this book?) the old presenter's adage, "Tell them what you're going to tell them, tell them, then tell them again".

It's easy to overlook these pearls of wisdom, so let's have a closer look.

Listen to the speeches of Presidents and Prime Ministers and you'll notice that their key points come in groups of three. Why is that? Well, we don't really know why, but we do know that it works. For some reason, groups of three sound good, feel good and they're easy to remember.

Groups of three are:

☑ Enjoyable

☑ Memorable

☑ Convincing

Memories are Made of This

Do you remember this?

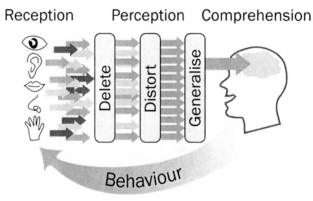

Reception   Perception   Comprehension

One of the important things to understand about your senses and therefore the process of learning is that your senses are differential. They are sensitive, not to the level of a stimulus but to a change in the level of that stimulus.

6.1 Spot the Difference

Place your left hand, palm down, on a table top or similar surface. Carefully press the tip of your right index finger against the back of your left hand. Be sure to hold your hands very still. How long is it before you no longer feel the pressure?

Stare at the + in this image for thirty seconds, then look at a white surface. What do you see?

What does this tell you about how to make your pitch stand out from the background noise?

Our senses are designed for new experiences, for novelty. Our perceptions, which follow our senses, notice novelty. Our memories, which reflect our perceptions, are built upon novelty. We remember our first times, and we remember intense new experiences more clearly than everyday experiences.

If you can make multiple connections, the link between you and the client gets stronger. Reinforcing one connection has some value, for example if the client reads the same advert every month in the same magazine, but reinforcing the overall connection in different ways is far more powerful.

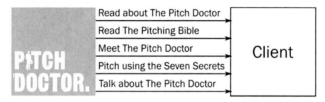

PITCH DOCTOR.	Read about The Pitch Doctor	Client
	Read The Pitching Bible	
	Meet The Pitch Doctor	
	Pitch using the Seven Secrets	
	Talk about The Pitch Doctor	

Do you remember this?

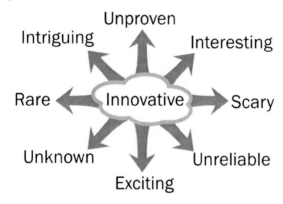

Imagine that, in your brain, you have a bucket full of memories. Each memory can be pulled out of the bucket and experienced by pulling on the appropriate string. The label lets you know what kind of memory it is, and the more labels that are attached to a memory, the easier it is to pull out.

We could say that the more labels a memory has, the stronger it is.

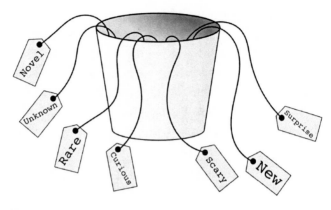

All of these labels are attached to the same memory; they are synonyms. You can take any of the strings and pull out the same memory.

What about memories that have very different labels?

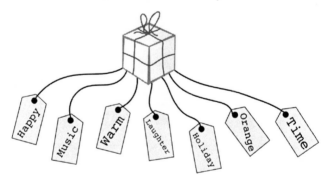

6.2 Memory labels

I'm going to give you a series of labels for memories. Each will bring a memory to mind. I want you to work though the list, one by one, starting with the first memory that comes to mind. If you can, stay with the same memory and explore deeper within it. If not, take the next memory that comes to mind. Just see where it takes you.

☑ A childhood memory

☑ The colour red

☑ A boy's name beginning with R

☑ A gift

☑ A feeling

What memories are evoked by these words?

What does that mean?

We make new memories by connecting new experiences to what we already know. When you introduce a new idea in your pitch, no matter how innovative or revolutionary it is, your audience can only make sense of it by comparing it to what they already know.

By connecting concepts and ideas together, by creating a chain or a journey, you create a series of foundations that lead the audience towards an outcome that is far more under your control.

Repetition, for our purposes, means passing the same message or information through as many of the audience's learning channels as possible.

Learning Styles

To make a decision, a client has to go through a process of learning. There are many theories of learning, including Kolb's 'learning styles' model, which gives us four 'preferences':

Activist

Likes to jump in and try something new. Always the first to volunteer for a demonstration. Give them something to do, a model or sample to play with. Get them involved.

Pragmatist

Likes to understand the 'right' way to do something. Seeks proof that something will work. Asks for case studies, evidence and references. Get them involved, and let them talk to other customers.

Theorist

Likes to know the theory, the way that it works. Seeks the evidence, the rules that govern success. Give them evidence and abstract models to prove that the thinking behind your idea is sound.

Reflector

Likes to stop, step back and think about an idea. Needs to mull it over and arrive at a more emotional conclusion. Give them time to think.

But how do you know which of these styles your audience prefers? No need – just provide something for each of them.

Holding Attention

During the pitch, the audience's attention naturally wanes. If the room is dark and the presenter's voice is a droning monotone, this process is accelerated.

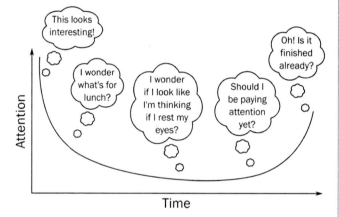

Either make your pitch so short that you have the audience's attention throughout, or break the pitch into a number of shorter sections.

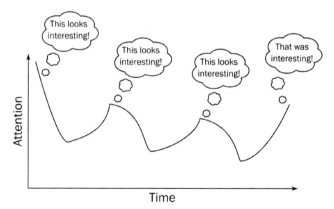

Recapture the audience's attention

☑ Reiterate what you said at the start of your pitch

☑ Ask the audience a few questions, encouraging a short period of interactivity

☑ Give the audience an interactive demonstration which builds up through a number of steps

☑ Pause and give the audience time to reflect

☑ Take a break and get some fresh air

☑ Bring in another speaker or a video

☑ Use words such as "now", "stop", "look", "bright", "quick" which tend to wake people up

People need time to reflect in order to process new information, so for the audience to really understand your pitch, you need to give them time to reflect. You literally need to pause for thought.

Pitch Blindness

If the client has seen pitches from a number of suppliers, they will all begin to merge into one. By mid-morning, the client won't be able to remember who said what, to who, about what.

Make sure you have the audience's attention, and that you have neutralised any other pitches they may have heard before starting your own.

"I know you've heard some other pitches today, and they're probably already starting to merge into one. So feel free to take a moment to clear your mind so that I can make sure I give you what you need to give me your full attention right now. Ready?"

If I've Told You Once...

I've told you a thousand times. It really doesn't matter how many times you tell me, you have to tell me, show me, get me to tell you, write it down, try it out, play with it, hold it, use it, buy it and then I might have some idea of what you're talking about.

When you have communicated your dream into your client's mind, you have to make sure it doesn't slip out again before you reach the all important part – the part where the client takes action.

Secret Brief

Make it Memorable

I saw a really great pitch once. I can't remember what it was about or who the company was, but it was very enjoyable.

That makes it a terrible pitch.

How many adverts can you remember where you have no idea what the product is that they're advertising?

Memories are Made of This

If you can understand how memories are formed and stored, you have a better chance of influencing what people remember, which means you have a better chance of influencing their decisions.

Learning Styles

In order to make a decision, the audience must absorb, organise and understand new information. This is essentially the process of learning, so by understanding different learning styles, you can organise your pitch to be more effective.

Holding Attention

It's not always realistic to hold the audience's attention throughout your entire pitch, however there are a number of ways that you can make more of a typical audience's attention span.

Pitch Blindness

When a client has seen too many pitches, they become pitch blind and you risk becoming part of the background noise. By standing out, you greatly increase your chances of being memorable and of influencing the client's decision.

SECRET 7

THE END
...OR IS IT?

The End?

What do you do at the end of your pitch?

Do you make for the door as quickly as you can, relieved that it's finally over?

Do you hang around like the last person at the party, talking to all the stragglers?

Do you make a grand exit?

Or do you try to slip out without anyone noticing?

You need to put as much effort into what you do at the end of your pitch as you put into planning and preparing for the start of it.

Why?

Well, what was the last film you saw at the cinema?

What was the first film you saw at the cinema?

What was the tenth film you saw?

There are many reasons why the end of your pitch is important, and why you must not leave the lasting impression that your clients have to chance, and this is just one of them.

We tend to remember the start and end of something more easily than we remember the middle. We remember the first instance of something and the most recent instance of it, and not much in between. This ties in with what we know about our senses; that they detect changes in information, not absolute levels. The first and last times we experience something mark a transition, and we are programmed to detect changes, or transitions, in the world around us.

How you begin and how you end your pitch are therefore potentially more important than what you say in the middle.

Now I'm not suggesting that you end with a song and dance routine, or fireworks, or some other grand finale, I'm just saying that your pitch has to have a clearly defined end. It cannot fizzle out when the audience has lost interest.

Your pitch will end when you say it ends.

Questions

"Thank you, that's the end of my pitch, do you have any questions?"

Have you ever said that?

It's so common that everyone does it, simply because it seems to make sense to take questions at the 'end' of your pitch. However, it creates problems.

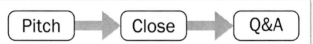

- ☒ Hand control back to the audience before you have finished
- ☒ Let the audience dictate the pace of questions
- ☒ Allow the audience to decide when there are no more questions
- ☒ Let the audience decide when the pitch ends
- ☒ Miss the golden opportunity to incorporate the questions into your summary
- ☒ Admit that you didn't cover everything
- ☒ Allow the pitch to fizzle out when time is up

What should you do instead?

The solution is very simple. Invite questions just before you are ready to summarise your pitch.

☑ Decide when the pitch ends

☑ Decide how many questions you want to answer

☑ Decide how long you want your answers to be

☑ Decide if you want to defer some questions to another time

☑ End right on time

☑ Hold the room until you're ready to hand it back

☑ Incorporate the questions and answers into your summary

☑ Show the audience that you anticipated and welcomed their questions

☑ Maintain control of the entire pitch from start to finish

"At this point I'd like to allow ten minutes for questions before I close my pitch. What questions do you have?"

Does a film end, or does it just fizzle out when the characters have nothing left to say?

In order for you to maintain control of your pitch, it has to end when you decide, not when the audience decides.

Why Do People Ask Questions?

☑ To demonstrate knowledge

☑ To demonstrate superiority over the presenter

☑ To disguise an objection

☑ To provoke a response from the presenter

☑ To provoke a response from another audience member

☑ To demonstrate attentiveness

☑ To waste time

☑ To set up for an attack

☑ To hide the fact that they weren't listening

☑ To gain control

☑ To learn something

Leading questions, or at least questions that are not motivated by a genuine interest in the answer, can lead you away from your intended direction and prevent you from getting your message across.

Handling Questions

Whether you're going to take questions throughout your pitch or just before your summary, you need to do these things:

Questions

☑ Allow time in your schedule – as a rule of thumb, plan your pitch to last about three-quarters of your allocated time.

☑ Handle questions using the format that I'm going to give you in a moment, otherwise you will get sidetracked, which dilutes your key message and eats up time

☑ Preferably have someone else manage the Q&A process for you to prevent you from getting drawn in to the questions

☑ Make a note of the questions so that you can incorporate your answers into the end of your pitch

ERR

Here's a simple way of handling any question to ensure you maintain control and answer only genuine questions.

Someone asks you a question.

You say, "Err..."

☑ Echo back their question

☑ Rephrase it to show you understand

☑ Reply if appropriate

> ### Echo

> ### Rephrase

> ### Reply

When you Echo back the question, the questioner can decide if that's what they really meant to ask you.

When you Rephrase the question, you give the questioner another chance to check that what you understand is what they meant. It also gives you a chance to check that the questioner's motives are genuine.

Reply, but only if you want to. You may choose to defer the question until later, if it breaks the flow of your pitch, or you may ask the questioner to ask it again when you get to the Q&A part of your pitch.

Panel Q&A

One person will have the role of 'chairman', managing the questions. Here's what they do:

1. Invite questions from the audience
2. Select someone to ask a question
3. Repeat the question so that the whole audience can hear it, and clarify it if necessary
4. Select a speaker to respond
5. Check that the answer is satisfactory
6. Move to the next person with a question or close the Q&A

You can see how steps 3 and 4 are partly designed to give the speaker time to think of a good answer!

When you're pitching in a team, one person manages the Q&A part of the pitch, leaving the rest of the team to handle questions and, importantly, record them for use in your follow-up.

When you're pitching by yourself, just remember to say "ERR".

Anticipating Questions

There will be certain questions that you can anticipate from the audience, so by addressing these in your pitch, you save time.

There's nothing to be gained in avoiding awkward questions, because to be asked the question puts the questioner in control. You maintain control by pre-empting awkward question, as you get to choose how and when you answer them. The audience will know when you've been 'caught off guard'.

Just Five More Minutes.... Pleeeeease

No matter how carefully you close your pitch, there's always a chance that someone in the audience will have saved their question for when they think you've finished. This might be because they've only just thought of it, or it might be because they want to upstage you.

When you say the pitch has ended, you hand control of the room back to the audience. Try one of these responses:

"I'm sorry, I've used all the time that you've given me for my pitch"

"If there are more questions, why don't we arrange another meeting, after we've all had time to reflect, so that we can discuss the way forward?"

Closing Your Pitch

Closing your pitch means much more than simply saying 'thank you' and running for the door.

The close serves three vital purposes:

☑ The close wraps up any loose ends from your pitch

☑ The close drives home your main message

☑ The close marks the point where you hand the room back to the audience

There are many ways that you can choose to close your pitch.

☑ A summary of the key message

☑ A call to action, as in the AIDA format

☑ Repeat what you said at the beginning of the pitch

☑ Refer to something that has been in the audience's view throughout your pitch, placed solely to engage their curiosity

☑ Fulfil a promise that you made at the start

☑ You could end just by saying "thank you"

What you're doing by closing your pitch is acknowledging that the client has given you an audience, literally, for your pitch, and so your pitch resides within your relationship with your client, and that relationship resides within your business world.

The Business World

Marking out your territory is important, and what is equally important is that you rescind that territory at the end of your pitch. This is the fundamental difference between an arrogant pitcher and a confident pitcher.

An arrogant pitcher acts like he owns the place

A confident pitcher knows that he owns the space

The space, the right to work within the territory, is a privilege granted by the client. You accept that privilege when you enter the room, and you hand the territory back when you leave. In between those two points, it is your responsibility to take good care of it.

Call to Action

The call to action is the key to your pitch, because it contains the very reason that you are pitching – your outcome.

Your call to action must give the audience a reason to act that is in their interests, and your pitch provides the means to achieve that result.

Closing the Loop

You'll find the description for this in Secret Three, so I won't repeat it. Suffice to say that you close the loop that you opened at the beginning of your pitch.

The Promise

As with Closing the Loop, you'll find the description for this in Secret Three.

You might promise that, by the end of your pitch, someone in the audience will have said a certain phrase. You have to be very confident in your pitch to try this, but it's definitely worthwhile when someone says, "If only we had bought this product last year..." and you pull the card out of the envelope to reveal those same words. It's just as effective when you combine it with pre-empting an awkward question, and the prediction reads, "This will never work..."

Thank You

The audience has given you their time and attention, and the least you can do is to acknowledge that with a sincere 'thank you'.

If you're planning an emotive, high impact ending, you might not want to lessen the impact by saying thank you afterwards, so say it before. For example, "I'm grateful for your time and attention today, and in closing I want to remind you that..."

Encore!

Your audience will metaphorically shout, "More!" by coming up to you at the end of your pitch with questions. If you've been giving an informative presentation, perhaps a lecture or a presentation at a conference, you'll find that the audience want to take away something to remember you by, perhaps a business card or book.

What's the encore to your pitch? Do you send a DVD with the video highlights? A thank you card? As an absolute minimum, you must send a follow up letter.

The seeds that you have planted in your pitch need watering. They need nurturing. Those ideas must be strengthened if they are to flourish into a fully fledged decision, a firm commitment to you and your product or service.

Follow up letters

A follow up letter is perhaps the most important post-pitch activity. As soon as the pitch is complete, make sure you make notes about key events, statements from the client, valuable questions and so on.

Use the key points from your pitch, and the audience's questions, in your follow up letter, and put it in the post on the day of the pitch, if possible. When the client receives the letter the next day, it creates a clear link between your pitch and your desire to work with them.

If the client has seen pitches from a number of suppliers, your follow up letter will help to make yours stand out.

There are no 'rules' for a follow up letter, so just remember to include:

Follow Up Letter

☑ A thank you for the audience's time

☑ The most important points of your pitch

☑ A reminder of what you want the reader to do

☑ The next step, should they make a favourable decision

☑ A sincere desire to continue building a professional relationship

In fact, if you follow any 'rules' or set format for a follow up letter, it could come across as a 'cut and paste' template, and that will do more harm than good.

Compare the following two letters. What effect do they have on you?

> JM Enterprises
> 1st January 2010
>
> Dear Tom,
>
> I'm writing to thank you for your time and hospitality on Tuesday when you gave me the opportunity to pitch our proposal for a new mouse trap to you and your team.
>
> We particularly valued your input on the packaging options and your ideas have now been incorporated into our marketing plan for the new design.
>
> I'd like to emphasise what I feel are the most valuable points of our proposal so that I can ensure you have what you need to make the right decision. To work with us would have the following benefits:
>
> We will reduce your time to market by 50%
> We will reduce your marketing costs by 20%
> We will increase Return On Investment by 30%
>
> If you decide to accept our proposal by Friday, we can be ready to begin work by the following Monday.
>
> I am available to answer whatever questions you and your team may have, and we are all looking forward very much to seeing you again and to working with you.
>
> With best regards,
>
> *Jerry*

TC Enterprises
1st January 2010

Dear Client,

Thank you for your attendance at our recent pitch.
It was very nice to see you there.

I trust that you obtained the information you needed
from it and I look forward to receiving your decision
at your earliest convenience.

I would like to take this opportunity to remind you
that TC Enterprises is the leading manufacturer of
products to the mouse catching industry, with
production facilities in eight countries and an
annual turnover in excess of $10,000,000. With
local support offices in 26 countries, you can be
assured of our personal attention at all times.

Yours Faithfully,

Tom

A follow up letter is an extension to your pitch. It drives home the key message, keeps your pitch fresh in the clients' mind and creates a bridge to your next meeting.

Even if your pitch is not successful, you can at least expect detailed and objective feedback from the client. Remember that every pitch is an opportunity to learn, and your audience is your best teacher.

Thank You, You've Been a Wonderful Audience

Your pitch began long before you spoke your first word, and it ends long after you have said, "thank you" and closed your laptop.

This brings us to the end of Secret Seven and indeed to the end of the book.

I hope that, as a result of reading this book, you have realised that a pitch is much more than just another presentation. It is a unique opportunity to make a connection with your audience, to claim your space, to convey your hopes and dreams into your client's mind and to lead the audience on a rich, vivid, emotive journey that leads directly to the best result that you could hope for – a successful, fruitful and mutually rewarding business relationship.

Pitching is complex because people are complex. A single person is complex enough, but when you place a number of them together in a room and call them an audience, they begin to interact and behave in ways that you couldn't have imagined. Yet, overall, they have a compelling need to relate to you and to support you, because they have already given you their time in anticipation of a mutually rewarding result.

When you're pitching, you and your audience share a unique experience that will never happen again. That pitch, that moment is one of a kind.

Make every moment count. Make every pitch count.

Secret Brief

The End?

The pitch ends when the decision is made, and not before.

Questions

Take questions before you summarise so that you can incorporate them into your closing and maintain control until you've finished.

Why Do People Ask Questions?

It's rarely why you would like them to.

Handling Questions

ERR. Echo, Rephrase, Reply

Anticipating Questions

It's better to answer than to be asked.

Just Five More Minutes.... Pleeeeease

One more question? At your own peril...

Closing Your Pitch

However you close your pitch, the important thing is that you close it. Closing your pitch hands the room back to the audience and completes the marking of your territory.

- ☑ The close wraps up any loose ends from your pitch
- ☑ The close drives home your main message
- ☑ The close marks the point where you hand the room back to the audience

Encore!

What's your encore? As a minimum, a personalised follow up letter.

Thank You, You've Been a Wonderful Audience

No, really, I mean it. Remember to tip your waitress.

THE SECRETS 7 OF A PERFECT PITCH

The Seven Secrets

Secret 1: It's All About Them

You can solve any problem in your pitch by looking at it from the audience's point of view. Your outcome is for you, your focus is on your audience.

Principles

Secret 2: By The Time You Start, It's Already Too Late

The pitch begins the moment the audience buys the ticket.

Beliefs

Secret 3: Steady, Ready, Pitch

Make sure you have the audience's full attention before you begin, even if you spend most of the time getting it.

Outcome

Secret 4: Dream The Dream

Your pitch began as an idea, so convey that idea into a vivid, tangible reality within the audience's mind.

Meaning

Secret 5: Mind Your Language

Make the difference between a good pitch and a winning pitch by carefully crafting your language.

Content

Secret 6: Say It Again, Sam

To make a decision, the client has to go through a process of learning, so applying the basic principles of learning will make your pitch memorable and influential.

Secret 7: The End... Or Is It?

The pitch only ends when you get the result you want... the contract, the decision, the 'yes'.

I'm sorry to say that there isn't much to choose between you and your competitors. Their product, service, format or design may have slightly different features or qualities than yours, but that doesn't mean that one is better than the other. What it means is that one is *better suited to the client* than another.

The product is secondary to the pitch, and the pitch becomes the only way to get your message heard above the background noise of your competitors.

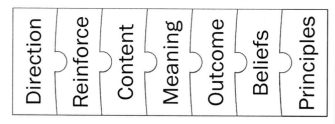

Now you can see how the Seven Secrets of a Perfect Pitch fit together, like the pieces of a jigsaw puzzle. Each Secret both builds upon and serves as a foundation for the others.

When you build your pitch around all Seven Secrets, the result will be far greater than the sum of its parts.

Each of these puzzle pieces takes your core message and elevates it to a position high above that of your competitors.

When you read, learn and apply these Seven Secrets, you give your pitch every chance to be an outstanding success.

Now that I have shared with you the Secrets that it has taken me 25 years to learn, the rest is up to you.

THE
APPENDIX

Acknowledgements

There are a few people who I would like to acknowledge and give a huge 'thank you' to for their part in the creation of this book.

To Sam and Henrietta - I love you - thank you for your support and inspiration

Sam - every day you teach me something new and much of your wisdom has found its way into these pages.

To my parents, Laszlo and Helen, for their continuing love and support and for teaching me the values that have held me in good stead throughout my life.

To Dr. Richard Bandler for his great knowledge and for developing the field of NLP. He has enriched my life and influenced many of the ideas and attitudes to be found both in this book and my trainings.

To Stewart Pearson and Les Hughes from STEEL London for their great eyes and advice.

To everyone at CGW Publishing for their continued professionalism and support.

To the colleagues and friends who have inspired and influenced my education and training over the years; especially Kate Benson, Owen Fitzpatrick and Dr Tim O'Brien. Also, due respect to Garner Thomson, John and Kathleen La Valle and The Society of NLP.

Paul Boross

London

April 2012

NLP References

Dr Richard Bander has kindly given me his written permission to reproduce some of his ground-breaking work on NLP within this book.

The following exercises and section draw upon the body of knowledge of Neuro Linguistic Programming and I gratefully acknowledge Dr Bandler's valuable contribution to this book.

Secret Two: From PITCH to BIBLE

P	I↓	T	C	H
P	A	T↓	C	H
P	A↓	R	C	H
P	E	R↓	C	H
P	E	A	C	H↓
P	E	A	C↓	E
P	E	A↓	S	E
P	E↓	R	S	E
P↓	U	R	S	E
B	U↓	R	S	E
B	I	R	S↓	E
B	I	R↓	L	E
B	I	B	L	E

Paul Boross

The Pitch Doctor is Paul Boross - psychologist, author, performer, musician, NLP trainer, public speaker, corporate strategist and internationally recognised authority on communications, presentation, performance and "the art and science of persuading people to give you business".

Drawing on a career that has seen him move from primetime TV and stand-up comedy to trans-Atlantic development deals, media consultancy and motivational psychology, Boross has worked with such power players as the BBC, Google, The Financial Times, Royal Bank of Scotland and MTV, training executives from the worlds of business and media in a range of communication, presentation, storytelling, performance and pitching skills. He has also worked with several household names, including Virgin chief Sir Richard Branson, TV chef and comedian Ainsley Harriott, and Sky newscaster Dermot Murgnahan.

Combining humour and motivational psychology, Boross is much in demand as a speaker at international television events, including MIPTV in Cannes, the Kristallen Swedish TV awards in Stockholm and the BCWW programming market in Seoul. He also lectures regularly for the Entertainment Master Class, the prestigious executive education programme for the international entertainment industry.

Boross' approach to pitching and presenting - described by the Daily Express as "a master class in verbal communication" - has now been distilled into a number one Amazon best-selling book, The Pitching Bible: The Seven Secrets of a Successful Pitch, which sets out his proven techniques for "getting your message across, every time".

Boross' frontline experience of performance - he is the resident motivational psychologist on Sky's hit series School Of Hard Knocks with English rugby icon Will Greenwood and counts a 12-year stint at London's legendary Comedy Store among his credits - coupled with a strong commercial grounding has given him rare insight into the entertainment world's distinctive pressures, pitfalls and potential.

His television credits also include presenting the primetime BBC2 series Speed Up Slow Down, which focused on time management and psychology; a guest spot in ITV's Wannabe, advising young people on the psychology of breaking into the TV and music businesses; and appearances on BBC1's The Politics Show.

www.thepitchdoctor.tv

The Pitching Bible

Discover the original Pitching Bible;

The Pitching Bible

ISBN 978-0-9565358-2-5

CGW Publishing

The Consulting Room

Visit www.thepitchingbible.com for more ideas and for resources that you can download and use when you're preparing your pitches.

Contacting The Pitch Doctor

You can contact The Pitch Doctor by email at:

info@thepitchdoctor.tv